OUTPERFORM THE NORM
for TRIATHLON

50 Best Tips EVER for Swimming, Biking & Running

SCOTT WELLE | *#1 Best Selling Author*

Copyright © 2019 by Outperform The Norm

For permission requests, speaking inquiries, and bulk order purchase options, email speaking@scottwelle.com.

All rights reserved. No part of this publication or the information in it may be quoted from or reproduced in any form by means such as printing, scanning, photocopying or otherwise without prior written permission of the copyright holder.

This book is not intended as a substitute for the medical advice of physicians. The reader should regularly consult a physician in matters relating to his/her health and particularly with respect to any symptoms that may require diagnosis or medical attention.

Terms of Use: This is a work of nonfiction. Nonetheless, the names, personal characteristics of the individuals, and details of the events have been changed to disguise identities or protect the privacy of the author's clients and students. Any resulting resemblance to persons living or dead is entirely coincidental and unintentional.

Effort has been made to ensure that the information in this book is accurate and complete, however, the author and the publisher do not warrant the accuracy of the information, text and graphics contained within the book due to the rapidly changing nature of science, research, known and unknown facts and internet.

I don't believe in "magic pill" programs - only in dedication, perseverance and hard work. You alone are the variable and are accountable for the results you get in your life, and by reading this book you agree not to attempt to hold me liable for your decisions, actions or results, at any time, under any circumstance.

ISBN: 978-1070821207

2nd edition, March 2019

Printed in the United States of America

To the triathletes with whom I've been privileged to work –
thank you for driving me crazy while simultaneously
making me a better coach.
I appreciate you!

BULK DISCOUNT PROGRAM FOR TRIATHLON TEAMS

Lead or manage a triathlon team?
Want to help them Outperform?
Consider purchasing this book and the supplementary resources
so they can train AND race smarter, faster, and injury free.

Please contact scott@scottwelle.com to discuss bulk pricing options.

Want to get even more out of this book?
It's 100% Absolutely Free

THE TRIATHLON VIDEO VAULT

The Triathlon Video Vault is a collection of multimedia resources geared towards helping you swim, bike and run smarter, faster, and injury free. It includes:

- ✓ The BIG Key to Swimming Efficiently
- ✓ How to go 1-2 mph Faster on the Bike Immediately
- ✓ Preventing Overuse Injuries in Triathlon
- ✓ 3 Essential Elements to Racing your Best
- ✓ Time Trialing and Performance Improvements
- ✓ 4 Keys to Beat the Heat in Training & Racing
- ✓ Heart Rate Training the Physiology of Recovery
- ✓ Mastering Your Triathlon Transitions

FREE INSTANT ACCESS AT:
OutperformTheNorm.com/books

C'mon in. Triathlon is a lot easier on the inside.

INTRODUCTION

Triathlon is an amazing sport that has changed my life. I say this for a number of reasons. First, there's the obvious social component. I love the camaraderie and getting out there, training with friends and fellow triathletes. There's being with Mother Nature, embracing the fresh air and everything that she has to offer. There's the simple variety aspect of triathlon. Life can get boring, monotonous and mundane when you feel like you're doing the same thing over and over and over again (which can pretty easily happen if you're doing a single sport such as running or cycling or swimming) and having a mix of three sports keeps it interesting. I also firmly believe that triathletes are the fittest people on the planet. Aesthetically speaking, they have the best bodies. Look at the start line of any triathlon and you'll see what I mean. Swimming broadens the shoulders, develops the back muscles and builds rotational core power. Cycling tones the leg muscles and triceps (from holding yourself up on the bike). Running develops the calves and sheds unwanted body fat so you have the fit, lean look that many people desire. The aesthetic part of the body is simply a byproduct of this cross-training fitness.

I have no idea why you've come to this book. Maybe you are someone who is looking to get into triathlon and you don't know where to begin. Or maybe you're someone who has done a few triathlons and you want to go the next level by being maximally efficient and effective with what you're doing.

This book will give you both answers.

As far as my background in triathlon – I always tell people that I'm a basketball player turned wanna-be endurance athlete. I simply say this because I don't have a background in any of the three sports. Growing up, I was the kid that was held back in swimming lessons and wasn't allowed to go into the deep end of the pool. I couldn't do "the crawl," (what most people know as "freestyle"). I had to constantly keep my head above water and do a modified doggy-paddle because I couldn't breathe. I was one of the worst swimmers in my class. Also, I didn't own a bike growing up and I only really ran if someone was chasing me. I was football player, basketball player and golfer. I drifted in triathlon not knowing what the heck I was doing.

My first endurance race was the Atlanta Marathon (a little over ten years ago). I knew I wanted to do a marathon at some point because it was on my bucket list, but I thought that it would be *one and DONE*. I thought I would do the race, check it off the list, leave it alone and never come back to it. But that marathon changed everything for me. It spurred me into triathlons and, fast-forward to the present, where I've completed five Ironman Triathlons and 23 marathons. Life takes crazy turns.

The take-home point of this story is if I can do it, *anyone* can do it. Even YOU can do it…I guarantee it! A lot of the tips in this book are based on my own person struggles. I had to figure these things out because of my lack of background in triathlon. It was trial and error and my own experimentation to find out what was going to work best for me. Then, I took that information, tested and refined it, and I'm passing it along to you in a way that will allow you to maximize your time, energy, fitness and enjoyment in this great sport.

Doesn't that sound nice?

What keeps many people from getting into triathlons is the time commitment. Variety is great but you also have to find a way to be able to balance it in your everyday life. I know, specifically, from a lot of the clients with whom I've worked that it can be very difficult to swim and bike when you're traveling (or just busy in general). You have to find a pool or a lake and you're probably not going to pack your bike and travel with it. It requires an awful lot of planning. Even if you don't travel, you have to think about how you're going to structure triathlon training against your day-to-day responsibilities in life, personally and professionally. It is important to find balance because it will make or break your training.

More than anything, I am going to give you strategies that will help you focus on QUALITY, instead of quantity. THAT is what I'm about when I work with people. It's about showing them the most efficient, effective way to get from point A to point B. This book gives you 50+ tips that cover everything from swimming, to biking, to running, to mindset, to performance nutrition. Most people think triathlon is three sports – it's not. It's FIVE sports. And because of my background in sport psychology, we will talk about the mental side of triathlon, not only from staying motivated on a daily basis in training, but also the mental side of racing to be able to perform your best when it matters most. Lastly, you'll find additional bonuses for navigating transitions, "best in class" apparel choices and race specific strategies. We are going to cover it ALL...from A to Z.

Let's get started!

CONTENTS

INTRODUCTION 5

SWIMMING 10
    1. Form First 11
    2. Breathe Bilaterally 12
    3. Minimize Kicking 13
    4. Stay Calm and Breathe 14
    5. Practice Off Strokes 15
    6. Practice Drafting 17
    7. Sight More Often 18
    8. Warm Up 19
    9. Hold Your Own and Move Forward 20
    10. Practice Conditions Mirror Performance Conditions 21

BIKING 23
    11. Get a Good Bike Fit 24
    12. The Right Cadence 26
    13. Relax but Keep the Core Engaged 28
    14. Practice Gearing 28
    15. Take the Free Speed 29
    16. Stay Aero 31
    17. Single Leg Drills 32
    18. Body Weight on the Pedals 33
    19. EHI's 36
    20. Cost-Effective Cycling 37

RUNNING 39
    21. Cadence is King 40
    22. Key Areas to Stretch 42
    23. Relax Your Hands 43
    24. Train on Soft Terrain 44
    25. Quality over Quantity 47
    26. Do Brick Runs 49

27. Proper Pacing 50
28. Equalize Your Effort 53
29. Do Strides 54
30. The Big Three Workouts 55

MINDSET 57
31. Own The Commitment 58
32. Remove Self-Imposed Limitations 59
33. Set Performance Goals 60
34. Mustering Motivation 64
35. Monitor Your Mood 65
36. Expect the Best - Prepare for the Worst 66
37. Know Your Purpose 67
38. Make the Most of Your Potential 69

PERFORMANCE NUTRITION 71
39. Art and Science 72
40. The Foundational Layer 73
41. Getting Lean and Mean 75
42. No Low Carb Diets 76
43. Fuel Up and Keep Up 78
44. Hydration and ElectrolyteS 80
45. Recover to Build Up 85

THE FINISH LINE 88
46. The Importance Of Sleep 89
47. The Importance of Massage 90
48. Transitions 91
49. Your Transition Plan 94
50. Soak It Up and Pay It Forward 95

APPAREL & EQUIPMENT 97

TERMINOLOGY 105

ABOUT THE AUTHOR 113

ALSO BY SCOTT WELLE 115

SECTION 1

SWIMMING

"Do you want to be a pontoon or a speedboat?
Be efficient."

1. FORM FIRST

Form matters more in swimming than in anything else you'll do triathlon (much more so than biking or running). The simple reason this is the case is because water is about a 1000x denser than air. This means that if you have poor form when you're swimming, from an energy expenditure standpoint, you're going to be wasting *much* more gas than anybody else out there.

Sometimes people think that "practice makes perfect," but practice doesn't make perfect. Practice makes *permanent*. Remember that. The single best tip I can give you in regards to swimming, especially if you're getting started, is to focus on *perfect practice*. Perfect practice makes perfect, and perfect practice makes permanent as well.

I see a lot of triathletes who get out there and plow through the sets they are supposed to be doing for a workout. They think, "I'm supposed to swim 2000 meters," or, "I'm supposed to swim for 45 minutes," and all they care about is completing the workout. Well, if you're focusing only on *duration* or *distance*, and you're not focusing on the *form* that goes into that duration or that distance, you could be perfectly practicing poor form. That's not what you want.

Smart investments are to join a Masters swim group or hire a swim coach, to make sure you're doing the right things (especially in the beginning). It's going to pay off for you, big time, in terms of proper form and decreased energy expenditure.

2. BREATHE BILATERALLY

Bilateral breathing is important because it balances out your stroke. You're always going to have one side that it feels more comfortable for you to breathe on. It's like writing or eating with your right or left hand – it's always going to feel easier with one specific hand. Swimming is no different.

What happens, though, if you're always breathing on one side, is you'll start to pull more from that side. You won't even notice it's happening but when you start doing open water swims, you'll realize that you *thought* you were swimming straight because you could follow the pretty black line on the bottom of the pool, but now you look up in the lake and realize you're swimming waaay to the right, or waaay to the left. Your stroke isn't balanced and this is why breathing bilaterally is so important.

Even if it feels uncomfortable at first, when you're breathing on both sides, you're pulling equally from both arms. You can be assured that when it gets time to swim in open water and you don't have the black line at the bottom of the pool to navigate you, you'll be fine. The shortest distance between two points is always a straight line and "Army Swimming" (left-right-left-right-left-right) is not the optimal strategy for triathlon swimming ☺

3. MINIMIZE KICKING

All of triathlon is a game of energy and energy *management*. One sport stacks up on the sport that preceded it. When we talk about energy, you have to not only be able to get through the swim...but then bike after that...and run after that. There's a cumulative fatigue that goes into each sport that makes it difficult. You have to do whatever you can on the swim and the bike to conserve your energy so you can use it at the end (when it matters most).

To conserve your energy, you must *minimize your kicking* when you're swimming. The reason I say this is because you have to use your legs when you're cycling and running, and it doesn't make sense to fatigue them with a lot of kicking and wasted motion.

OUTPERFORMING TIPS

First, the reason that it's important to minimize kicking is because most swimmers (unless you have a background in swimming) are inefficient kickers. It's a huge energy waster. You're using the largest muscle group in your body (the legs) and you're going to be expending a large amount of energy, with a very small return in terms of propulsion. It makes sense to minimize kicking and save your energy, even if it means going slightly slower (and, I emphasize the word *slightly*) on the swim.

The other thing that negates the amount of kicking that you need to do is the fact that you're probably going to be wearing a wetsuit. If you're new to the sport, or if you've never worn a wetsuit before, they are the great equalizer in triathlon. Wetsuits take your body and put it on top of the water. It makes *everybody* buoyant. What you can do once you're wearing a wetsuit is to focus more on pulling from your upper body, and core, instead of worrying about what's going on with your legs. A lot of times, people feel the need to kick a lot because they feel like they're drowning. It's wasted energy to keep you from sinking instead of using that energy for propulsion and to keep you moving forward.

Minimize kicking and save your energy. Trust me, you'll feel it later in the race.

4. STAY CALM AND BREATHE

Swimming is about finding your rhythm. If you're new to the sport, you probably think swimming fast is mostly about fitness, especially if you get easily winded and tired when you're swimming. It's NOT about fitness. What people don't realize is they're very inefficient in their breathing.

The difference in swimming is that your head is face down in the water, as opposed to being up when you're cycling and running, where you can breathe whenever you want to. You don't have that luxury in swimming. It's much more about *timing* and *rhythm*.

Everybody from new swimmers, to more advanced swimmers, can benefit from dong simple breathing exercises, calming down and finding their rhythm when they're swimming. It's simply about finding the sweet spot of breathing that's in sync with what's going on in our stroke. One of the things I do, even after five Ironman triathlons, is to go over to the side of the pool and hang onto the side with one arm, relax my head into the water and focus on pivoting and swiveling my head to the side and breathing. All I'm focusing on is staying CALM, finding a rhythm, taking deep breaths, but breathing in and out like I would when I'm doing my regular stroke. This has worked for a lot of other people as well. Being able to find this sweet spot on the side of the pool helps to get comfortable, and it's something you can't necessarily find when you're swimming with others in a lane or in open water.

As simple as this may sound to you, it is a key aspect to being able to swim your best. From a physiology standpoint, your muscles need oxygen and your ability to swim your best (and fastest) is directly related to the amount of oxygen you can get into your heart and lungs, and then out to your working muscles. And if there are any inefficiencies in your breathing patterns (holding your breath, or short, shallow breaths), it's going to affect your ability to swim your best. Sometimes getting back to the basics and focusing on the *simple* fundamentals, as far as staying calm and breathing, can have a much BIGGER impact on your swim performance than most people realize.

5. PRACTICE OFF STROKES

You might be wondering why you should practice off strokes when you're not going to use them in triathlon? There are a couple of key reasons why. The first is to make your stroke more balanced and make you more comfortable in the water. That's part of the reason that you do it. The high level swimmers will all talk about having a good "feel for the water," and with water being 1000x denser than air, having a greater feel for the water and awareness of how your body moves through space is critically important to being able to swim your best. Doing different off strokes enhances this feeling and ultimately makes you a better swimmer.

Second, there will probably come a time when you're doing a triathlon where you have to throw in a couple of off strokes, particularly a breast stroke or potentially even a back stroke (if you've never done a triathlon, you'll understand what I mean after you've done one). It doesn't matter if it's a sprint, Olympic, 70.3 or an Ironman, you'll probably get to a spot where there are a lot of people around you and some chaos going on in the water. You need to calm and collect yourself a bit so you're able to swim your best. This is very difficult to do for newer swimmers if you try to continue on with the freestyle. You find that there are too many people around you. It has happened to me before too. You get a little nervous and rattled, and sometimes you need to peel it back, refocus and collect yourself, particularly with strokes where you don't have to worry about breathing.

The main thing that rattles people in triathlon swimming (other than having people around you) is swallowing water. Trust me, I've done it in open water swims, both in training and also in the race. That's usually what gets people the most, when you swallow a big mouthful of water and then you're trying to cough it out (sorry if this is disgusting you, but you deserve to know the truth!). You still have to continue to move forward, so practicing some off strokes when you're in the pool will greatly enhance your feel for the water and ability to pull it off in the open water. It gives you the necessary time to regroup and minimize any time lost before you get back to freestyle.

6. PRACTICE DRAFTING

Most people think of drafting in cycling, but the same principle applies in swimming as well. You can get in the wake (think of the wake of a boat) of somebody swimming in front of you and save an enormous amount of energy, simply by drafting and by being on their feet.

It's something you must *practice*. You can practice it in the pool AND practice it in the open water. It helps you not only from the energy saving standpoint, but you also don't have to worry about sighting as much. You can *slightly* look up and think about staying in that person's wake and on their feet. It lessens the pressure on you to swim in the straight line.

By practicing, you will become comfortable being close enough to someone where you can stay in their draft, but not so close that you're hitting their feet and ankles and legs with every single stroke you take. If you do that, you're going to get kicked (yes, I'm speaking from personal experience). There's a fine line to swimming close enough to gain a draft but not so close that you're on top of the person. If you're going to gain the benefits from drafting, it's important to find the appropriate distance so you can also settle into the rhythm to maintain your own individual stroke.

7. SIGHT MORE OFTEN

Sighting is what we refer to in triathlon as making sure that you're swimming in the correct direction. Obviously, again, when you're in the pool, you have the little black line that navigates you and keeps you going in the right direction. You don't have this luxury when you're swimming in the open water of an actual triathlon. You have to sight when you're swimming in the open water and remember that the shortest distance between two points is a *straight line.*

I can tell you from personal experience that the Ironman distance swim is 2.4 miles, but I guarantee you I've swam 2.6 or 2.7 miles because I've been zigzagging all over the place. It's definitely NOT the most efficient way to swim your best. Zigzagging is easy to let happen, especially when you get in the heat of the race. Sighting correctly and sighting often is a key aspect to triathlon.

When it comes to sighting, most people will lift their head up way too high and will lift their upper body as well. You have to understand what impact this has in the water. If you lift up too much, your legs are going to sink. Head comes up, legs go down.

What you want to focus on when you are sighting is lifting the minimal amount, knowing that any excess lifting will create drag and make you work harder. What you want to think about when you're sighting is *barely* lifting your head up and, unless you're swimming somewhere where you have huge massive waves that you're going to need to look over the top of, you'd be surprised how little you actually need to lift your head to be able to see the buoys and your sight lines to continue to swim straight.

So, in addition to barely lifting your head, think about sighting *more often*. Usually I will count a number, where I sight roughly every 10 strokes. I sight more often right after the gun goes off and the race has started. I will sight more often initially to make sure that I get started on the correct line when there's more chaos and people are more tightly packed, and then as things thin out, I will sight a little less often. Once I establish my direction that I'm going in I don't feel the need to sight quite as often. I'd recommend using the same strategy.

8. WARM UP

Warming up is key to getting your body ready for the race. It surprises me how few people will actually get into the water and do a very short warm up swim. This is actually not as much to warm up your swimming muscles, as it is to get acclimated to the water, and to get comfortable. It's a key aspect because when the gun goes off, you have to be ready to go. It doesn't matter if the race has an open water start or a beach start. You want to know what the water feels like and be as comfortable as possible when the race starts.

It doesn't have to be a long warm up – it can be something simple where you go off to the side from where the people are starting (most races will have some type of start where they'll be doing it either by age group or by gender). Take five solid minutes to kick your legs out a bit (to get them warmed up), do a few off strokes (along with freestyle), get calm, get comfortable and get composed in your breathing. Having this sense of security makes a big difference when the race starts.

9. HOLD YOUR OWN AND MOVE FORWARD

If you never really done triathlons before, the swim is a very interesting experience when you first get started, especially if you're doing an open water start to a race where people are treading water around you, and then they blow a cannon, or a gun, to start the race and everybody goes off at once. It's a little less chaotic if they do a beach wave start, but at the start of *any* triathlon, it barely even feels like swimming. I would call it more of a *royal rumble* in the water. It is easy to get kicked and hit when you're swimming. It's going to happen and you have to be prepared for it. No matter how much you try to avoid people, you're going to get kicked at some point and you're going to have somebody hitting your legs. In one Ironman I got my goggles completely knocked off my head!

I don't say this to scare you. You can easily avoid it and stay well off to the side, but it's going to be a *really* long swim if you do. I'd rather prepare you for what's to come, and this means staying calm, cool, collected and composed.

OUTPERFORMING TIPS

First, you *have to* swim strong and you have to hold your own. When the race starts, fight for your position. You have your own personal space when you're swimming, and no one gets to come into that personal space unless you *let them* come into your personal space. Remember that. Newer triathletes will normally be so freaked out by having other people around them that every time they get hit they'll bow out and swim to the side, and not try to hold their own. I'm not telling you to go out aggressively punching people but you need to be confident and own your personal position when you're swimming in the water.

Second, you always want to continue to move forward. That probably sounds easy, but it's not. In cycling, you can coast and you'll still be moving forward at *some* velocity. If you stop running, you can walk and you'll still be moving forward. But when you quit swimming, it's easy to stop and start treading water. When you do that, you're not moving forward at all. This was part of the reason that I brought up the importance of off strokes before because, even if you're not moving forward at the same velocity that you would be when you're doing freestyle, at least you're still *moving forward*! It doesn't matter if this off stroke is a breast stroke or back stroke or side stroke or a modified doggy paddle (I've done them all), as long as you are moving forward in some capacity, you're going to be a lot better off.

10. PRACTICE CONDITIONS MIRROR PERFORMANCE CONDITIONS

This is a critical aspect that we always used to talk about when I was doing sport psychology – whatever you're training for, you have to, as closely as possible, simulate the race specific demands in training so you get the carry-over from training to racing. Preparation breeds familiarity and familiarity breeds confidence.

If you are doing a specific type of triathlon where you know the water is going to be choppy, you have to find a way to mirror that in your practice conditions when you're training. Don't let the first time that you swim in choppy water be when the actual triathlon starts. You have to find a way to make it happen.

Same type of thing as what I've discussed in the last couple of points where, if you know that it's an open water start and there is going to be some chaos when the swim starts, go recruit some fellow triathletes and do open water swims where you "practice" getting hit and kicked around a little bit (within reason). Do this, and you'll be more comfortable when the race starts.

You also have to think about it from a nutrition and apparel standpoint as well. Whatever you're going to eat/drink in the race, you have to eat/drink in training. Whatever you're going to wear in the race, you want to wear it in training. Don't buy a new wetsuit and use it for the first time in the race. Same thing with a new pair of goggles. I see new triathletes do this all the time. They'll buy a brand new pair of goggles at the race expo the day before the race and use them. It ends up being a disaster! The goggles don't fit or they don't have right tint or they get water in them. I see it happen all the time.

You've got to dance with whom you brought to the party. Whatever you do in practice, it has to mirror what you're going to do when you need to perform. It's going to help your confidence and psyche tremendously on race day.

SECTION 2
BIKING

"Riding or hiding?
There is no substitute for time in the saddle."

11. GET A GOOD BIKE FIT

In triathlon, biking is your most time consuming sport. Because you're spending more time on the bike, it's imperative that you have the correct bike with the correct bike *fit*. As far as selecting the right bike, the most important thing is to buy a bike from a quality bike dealer. They should look at the length of your legs and limbs (and possibly even your flexibility) to select exactly what size bike you should ride on, whether it's a road bike or a triathlon bike.

Personally, I rode on the wrong size bike for a looong time. I won't say the brand of bike but the frame was simply too long. I had it refitted and had the stem shortened and, even with these alterations, it was still too long for me. I was in an outstretched position for my first two Ironmans and this put unnecessary stress on my shoulders. In the aerobars, I was uncomfortable and strained (when I should have been relaxed) and it hurt my cycling. Had I bought the correct bike for my body type and my limb length to begin with, it would have saved me loads of problems...and energy.

After you've selected the right sized bike, find someone who is a quality bike fitter that can fit you appropriately for your bike. Look at it like it's a tailor for clothes. If you're going to get your clothes tailored (whether we're talking about shirts, pants, suits, dresses or anything else), you want to go to a quality tailor because they are going to do the best job. Bike fitting is exactly the same way. If something fits you a little bit off or is too tight or too loose, you're not going to look and feel as good. So, whomever you go to for bike fitting, make sure they have a solid reputation. They should be tinkering around with a lot of different things, namely your positioning on the bike, how high or low your seat is (and forward or backward), the angle of your seat, how high or low your handlebars are, the angle of your handlebars, and the length of the stem on your bike. It all MATTERS. You're going to be spending hours on that thing – you may as well be as comfortable as possible.

You also want them to take a look at your biking shoes. Your cleat position is going to be a big determinant of the amount of power you generate in your pedal stroke. Usually, if you have your cleats back a bit farther on your shoes, your calf is going to be held in a more fixed position and your cadence will be lower, but typically you will be able to generate more power with each pedal stroke. Contrast this with having your cleats positioned more forward, where you'll be using the calf muscles more in your pedal stroke, your power will be a bit less, but your cadence is going to be higher (a good thing – discussed later). There isn't a right or a wrong way – you have to find what feels best to you.

Everybody has their own unique position (in terms of what is the most comfortable) for them when they're riding. Make sure you have it dialed in from the start! You don't want to be training on the wrong size bike or with the wrong bike fit for months when you're getting ready for a race. In cycling, inches and subtle changes matter and only *perfect* practice makes *perfect*. Otherwise, you're ingraining poor habits.

12. THE RIGHT CADENCE

Cadence is the most important factor in cycling performance (it may arguably be the most important in running as well). Biking with a high cadence is a key factor in your overall cycling ability because of what's going on inside of your body. Remember, everything stacks on itself when you're doing triathlon and there is accumulated level of fatigue that builds as you go forward. You want to not only conserve as much energy as possible when you're cycling so you have that energy to be able to cycle faster, but you also want to conserve that energy so you'll have more gas in the tank for running afterwards.

I'd consider lower cadences, in terms of RPMs (or *Revolutions Per Minute*), to be anything under 80 RPMs. When you're out riding, it may feel that you're able to go faster at this cadence and it's where you're supposed to be, but it's NOT. We call this *grinding a gear*. This lower cadence builds *more* fatigue in your legs. It also becomes difficult if you're cycling at a cadence of 80 RPMs for hours on end, to then get off the bike and start running at a cadence of 88-90 SPM (*Strides Per Minute*, the ideal number for running). Your body isn't going to want to match cadences.

I've read a lot on Lance Armstrong (please put aside the performance-enhancing drugs and everything else) and what a lot of people don't realize is that when he came back from cancer and was performing his best, he was better in the mountains in the *Tour de France* not only because he lost weight, but also because he changed his pedaling style. Chris

Carmichael coached him to do this for specifically this reason. Lance was always a guy that had a huge aerobic engine and a huge competitive desire, but he would spin at a very low cadence and grind through races. It resulted in a lot of residual fatigue in his legs. When he shifted to cycling and spinning with a higher cadence (90-105 RPMs), it put less overall fatigue in his body, and when he was doing multi-day stage races like the *Tour de France*, he had more gas in the tank for the later stages of the race (the same way that you'll have more gas in the tank and more energy for running). He became a more efficient cyclist.

For almost all triathletes, the sweet spot for biking cadence is 90-100 RPMs. If you don't have a cadence monitor on your bike where you're able to look at this, the easiest way to do it is to pick either your right side or your left side and count the number of pedal strokes you have for 20 seconds and multiply that number by three. So, if you're counting your right side and you count 30 RPMs for 20 seconds, then you multiply that by three and you'll know that you're spinning at 90 RPMs, which is an ideal cycling cadence. If it feels like you're spinning too fast, good. You're probably doing it correctly. But make sure you're shifted to the hardest gear where you can *comfortably* maintain a cadence of 90-100 RPMs.

Also, you want to constantly be monitoring your cadence on all different types of terrain, not only flats, but also uphills and downhills. Be aware of these numbers because it's going to have an impact on the fatigue in your legs and your cycling performance, as well as your energy level for the run.

13. RELAX BUT KEEP THE CORE ENGAGED

All high level athletes, whether in cycling, or running, or triathlon, or anything else, relax the muscles that DON'T need to be working. The involuntary muscles don't carry any excess tension or stress that aren't necessary and aren't useful in propelling them down the road. The core is the powerhouse of the body and all your energy comes from here. A strong tree is no good if it doesn't have strong limbs, right? Still, it's very easy to lose core integrity (or core strength) and this makes it very difficult to get the maximum amount of propulsion, force and intensity into your pedal stroke. You want to constantly be monitoring your level of core engagement as you're cycling.

If you're riding a road bike or a triathlon bike, many newbie cyclists will carry tension in their hands, arms and shoulders as they're cycling. Again, the best cyclists (and the best athletes) are able to relax the upper body, while the core, which is the "trunk of the tree," stays engaged. This will allow you to transfer more energy into the pedals and this will allow you to cycle, faster.

14. PRACTICE GEARING

Gearing on your bike is a *skill*. Like anything else, it's a skill that has to be learned and has to be practiced repeatedly. There is no hard and fast rule to gearing and there are a lot of different determinants to ride your best, depending on your level of strength, wind, terrain and the quality of the road. All these things factor into your chain ring and how you should gear your bike.

In general, your big ring (or your large chain ring) is most useful when you're riding downhill or downwind. The small chain ring is best used if you're riding uphill or into the wind. I see people make the mistake often, where they think they should be in the big ring, but cannot maintain a cadence of 90+ RPMs. They *should* be in the small ring and focus on spinning at a higher cadence. A lot of people think they are getting more out of being in a bigger ring, but they're not. They're excessively fatiguing their legs. The opposite thing happens when people ride downhill. They will be in the small ring and will be spinning a gear, even though it's not even helping them go any faster (they're not in a big enough gear). THAT is the time when you should drop it into the larger chain ring and allow the free speed and momentum to take over.

Practice gearing. There is no book on the market that can tell you *exactly* how to do it. You have to experiment with different grades, winds and quality of roads, but as long as you're focusing on maintaining a consistent cadence in a comfortable gear, you'll be fine.

15. TAKE THE FREE SPEED

Riding uphill and downhill are also SKILLS that need to be learned and practiced. I see a lot of newbies and recreational cyclists doing this *wrong*. I had to learn these skills the hard way as well. I'll never forget doing a race a few years ago called

"Horribly Hilly." It was 125-mile race in a hilly part of Wisconsin and it was the first time that I had ridden a lot of hills. Obviously, by the name of that race, *"Horribly Hilly"* was horribly hilly race, but I had no experience riding repetitive hills with cyclists that were a lot better than me. I always thought it would be about the quality of how fast I could go *uphill*, but I also realized the importance of being able to go downhill fast as well. I learned that downhill is the time to take the *free speed*. When you go over a hill, don't let up, stop pedaling and coast on the way down the hill. Instead, pop it into the big ring and pedal a few times (to take the speed) so when you're cresting a hill and going into a downhill, you can gain a lot of speed for very little energy expenditure. I see people many people make the mistake of climbing a hill and *crawling* over the top of the hill, and because they're tired, they coast and don't pedal on the back side part of the hill (usually, the downhill part). That's absolutely wrong. They're not maximizing their speed. They expend very little energy on the downhill and too much energy on the uphill. If you look at their heart rate graph when they're done (good indicator of energy expenditure) it will look like a jagged saw blade. It should look relatively flat.

Instead, focus on maintaining a high cadence. Don't worry about how fast you're going up the hill. From an energy standpoint, the energy it is going to take for you to go from 10 MPH to 12 MPH uphill is going to be much *larger* than it would take you to go from 25 MPH to 27 MPH on the downhill. Going from 25 MPH to 27 MPH would, literally, be you taking one pedal stroke and gathering a bit of momentum.

In terms of energy management in a triathlon, pay attention to taking the free speed on the downhills and not expending too much energy on the uphills. It's going to help you in the long run.

16. STAY AERO

When I say aero, I'm specifically speaking to people that have triathlon bikes with aerobars. In cycling, you need to think about the amount of resistance and friction from the wind. When you're cycling, you're traveling through air at a much faster speed than when you are running, so it makes aerodynamics all the more important.

Most people don't realize this, but your head is one of the biggest things that causes drag when you're cycling. You have to play around with what feels comfortable to you but, in general, you want to "tuck the head." Think about it like you're a turtle and you're trying to tuck your head *down* and *in*, because if you have your head sticking way out, it will catch a lot of wind. You might not think it makes a difference but it DOES. The time savings for biking 5 miles will be minimal, but if you're biking an Olympic distance, 70.3 or Ironman – it stacks up over time, and it can easily end up being *minutes* off of your time. You can have huge time savings if you play around with the position of your head.

This comes back to the same principle as practicing gearing on hills – it's all about *free speed*. Minimal energy, maximum returns. Professional cyclists spend hours in wind tunnels to reduce their drag and improve their aerodynamic profile. You don't need to go to these lengths but you do have to appreciate that anything that causes drag will slow you down and require more effort for you to travel the same distance.

17. SINGLE LEG DRILLS

Single leg drills are meant to balance out the dead spots in your pedal stroke so it's even and balanced. It's probably the single best drill that you can do to improve your cycling. A single leg drill involves having one leg unclipped from the pedals while cycling. Now, it probably makes sense that this is much better done when you're either on a spin bike or on an indoor trainer. You also don't want to be doing single leg drills for a long period of time. You'll quickly realize that they are more difficult than you think. If you haven't done them before, you'll see what I mean. They are only done for durations of 20-45 seconds. You want to be in a gear where you have a little bit of resistance and you're focusing on smoothing and balancing out the pedal stroke as much as possible.

If you are riding outside you can still do single leg drills. What you want to do to replicate doing this indoors is to simply *focus* on one leg. Focus on one leg for about 45-60 seconds, where you are really honing in on what's going on with your right leg and your right pedal stroke (and vice versa). *Just focus on that*. Does it feel like there are any dead spots in your pedal stroke? Does it feel like there are any inefficiencies? Then shift over to the left side and do the same exact thing. *Really* try to get in tune with what's going on in your pedal stroke!

This drill is best done in the warm-up and cool down. Shifting your focus to one side or the other and what's going on with your pedal stroke will be a huge determinant in how balanced, symmetrical and efficient you are as a cyclist. This is one of the things that high-level cyclists do much better than amateurs. They get more out of each pedal stroke and they don't waste any energy going into the pedals. They're like a sleek sports car. They get more miles per gallon out of each pedal stroke than a recreational cyclist.

Single leg drills are a basic fundamental to pay attention to, year round, to stay sharp. They can always help you.

18. BODY WEIGHT ON THE PEDALS

This concept single handedly changed my cycling performance. It's from a book called "*The Pose Method of Cycling*," and it probably added 1-2 MPH to my biking speed. Think about the distribution of your weight when you're biking. Poor cyclists will have all of their weight resting either on the seat, or on their handlebars. Your weight *should be* distributed on your pedals.

Next time you're riding indoors, stand up while you're biking. And after you stand up on the pedals, let go of the handlebars. You'll feel what it is like to have 100% of your body weight on the pedals. THAT is the feeling you want to mimic when you're biking.

Obviously, you're not going to ride standing up, without hanging on to your handlebars. But you want to get the feeling of your body weight being distributed as much as possible *on top of the pedals*. When you get this feeling, your cycling is going to go to an entirely different level.

You also want to think about your pedal stroke like a clock, where the majority of your power (or your weight) is being pushed down into the pedals from the 1 o'clock to the 4 o'clock position. That's the secret. Then, you do left-right, left-right, left-right, left-right, and that's what you focus on. It's almost like you're doing a little dance with the pedals. But it's in that 1 o'clock to 4 o'clock position where when you have your body weight on the pedals. That's where you're applying the force, and once you get past the 4 o'clock spot, your leg goes into "recovery mode" and is on autopilot (while the opposite leg is pushing down). It's like the other sports – there's a recovery mode when you're swimming as well, where one hand is catching and pulling the water and the other hand is recovering. Recovery in running happens after the pushoff in your stride. Cycling is exactly the same way. You always have an "active leg" that is pushing down while the other leg is recovering. Hopefully that makes sense.

Take home point here is to distribute as much of your body weight on top of the pedals and focus on *nothing else* other than pushing down from that 1 o'clock to the 4 o'clock position, and dancing with the left-right, left-right, left-right. If you can master this concept, it will explode your cycling performance.

BIKING

How To Go 1-2 MPH Faster On Your Bike IMMEDIATELY

Video describes exactly what to focus on when you're cycling and how to go faster on the bike *immediately*.

These are your keys to greater cycling efficiency.

Free Instant Access at:
OutperformTheNorm.com/books

19. EHI'S

This is the part where you start to think that I'm a slave driver but, EHIs are my term for what I call *"Excruciatingly Hard Intervals."* I've had many of my clients do these, and they produce great results. EHIs are very short, very intense intervals. They are usually less that 45 seconds. The reason that I have people do these is because we all get used to cycling at the same pace. It's much more difficult in cycling (more so than swimming or running) to hit certain speeds when you're riding outdoors, mostly because you have other things to worry about. You're watching the road, dodging traffic, managing the wind and the other riders around you, to name a few. There are more things going on in your mind that take away from focusing on your speed.

If you're swimming in a pool, you're easily able to monitor how fast you are swimming. Or if you're running on the track, you're easily able to calculate your paces and split times. EHIs take your cycling to another level because it gets you used to riding *faster* than you would ride on a daily basis.

To do EHIs, do 4-8 of them on any given ride. The intervals are only 40 seconds long and to start, pop it into a very difficult gear (definitely the big ring). Immediately stand up and hammer down on the pedals for 5-10 seconds to get up to speed, then sit back down (get into your aerobars if you're riding a triathlon bike). But you're focusing on a *very hard, very intense* interval for a *very short* period of time. When you stack these up and do them repeatedly for days and weeks and months on end, you will notice that you have more pop in your pedal stroke and you're able to push a harder gear than you're able to push right now.

Lastly, you always want to have plenty of recovery on these intervals as well. Try to have at least 2 minutes of recovery before you go into the next one. Continue to do EHIs over time and it will not only break up the monotony of riding in the same gear, at the same speed, all of the time, but it will also take your cycling performance to another level.

20. COST-EFFECTIVE CYCLING

Cycling is not a cheap sport. I've ridden with a lot of cyclists before who geek out over their bike and always want to have the latest model bike or the premium upgrades. You can pretty easily have a $5,000-$10,000 bike if you really want to. It's important to know what *really* matters in cycling performance.

I cringe when I see people throw down and buy carbon water cages or carbon stems that will save them a few *grams* of weight. Then this same person has an extra 5 or 10 *pounds* on their body frame. Does that make sense? Do the math. Does that *REALLY* make sense?

No, it doesn't.

For cost-effective cycling, don't get sucked into paying for the little things like that. If you're honestly interested in upgrading the performance of your biking (and I'm probably speaking to a more experienced triathlete here), the best thing you can do is to invest in is an aero helmet. This relates specifically to what I discussed in the sixth tip about being aerodynamic. An aero helmet, in terms of a dollar for dollar investment, is going to have the greatest return on the amount of speed that you get out of it. Nothing else compares. You can get a good aero helmet for anywhere from $80-$150. If you invest in nothing else other than an aero helmet, it will significantly benefit your race.

The next best thing (and this would certainly be more expensive) is to get race wheels. It's a friction thing. You'll not only have a deeper dish on the rim of your wheel (helps with aerodynamics), you'll also have less rolling resistance. If you think about it, the only point of contact between the bike and the ground is your tire (and, thus, your wheel), which is why race wheels have a massive influence on how fast you're ultimately able to go on the bike. You can spend anywhere from a few hundred to a couple of thousand dollars on race wheels. If you are looking to go as fast as you can, race wheels are a good investment. But it adds up quickly. In the grand scheme of things, since you're probably not going to be racing more than a few times a year, you have to decide whether it's worth that investment. Only you know the answer.

I do believe that an aero helmet is a great investment for any reasonably serious triathlete. And despite the distinct advantages of both of these upgrades, don't forget my original cycling point – it all starts with the right bike size and bike fit. That is, and always will be, the most important component in cycling.

SECTION 3
RUNNING

"Running is easy. But running after swimming and biking takes skill AND will."

21. CADENCE IS KING

The best triathletes are always the best runners. I've not only experienced this but I've also seen it first hand. The big reason this is the case is that there's the greatest opportunity to either gain time or lose time when you get to the run. You've got the residual and cumulative fatigue that stacks up throughout the course of the triathlon. Depending on the distance of your race, it can be a really long day out there. You're obviously *physically* tired by the time you get to the run, but you're also *mentally* (and sometimes *emotionally*) tired as well, depending on the conditions, heat/cold and wind. There's a huge opportunity to gain time if you manage the run very well and pace yourself properly, or a potential disaster for you to lose time if things don't go well in pacing and nutrition and mental toughness.

To be a good triathlete (and a good runner), it once again starts with cadence. I talked about this in cycling as well, but cadence is every bit as key when you're running as it is cycling, and it's key for a different reason. Because running is the only part of triathlon that's an *impact* sport, you have less "wiggle room" for inefficiencies in form. Current stats say that roughly 60% of all runners will get injured at some point throughout the course of a training year, and this happens because running is an *impact* sport with *impact* forces. Swimming isn't. Cycling isn't. So, you have to do whatever you can to minimize running impact forces as much as possible.

This comes back to your cadence and your overall running form. I always subscribe to the philosophy that people don't get injured because they *run* – people get injured because they run *wrong*. Their impact forces are too high and the pounding on their body causes too much wear and tear. Running in an economical way minimizes the amount of muscular damage on your connective tissues, tendons and ligaments. The body will always break down at its weakest link, and this is usually what happens over the course of time.

In running, you want to have a cadence of about roughly 88-90 SPM (*Strides Per Minute*). If you don't have a footpod or a device where you have real time monitoring of your cadence, you're going to need to count your foot strikes. Take either your right or left foot and count how many times that foot is hitting the ground in a 20 second period, and then multiply that number by 3. If you're at 29-30 in the span of 20 seconds, then you're at about 87-90 SPM, which is where you want to be.

A visual to focus on when you're running is to think about running on eggshells. Another one is to think back when you were younger and you ran next to the side of the pool (even though your parents probably told you not to). If there's water on the side of the pool, you had to take very short strides, and you had to make sure you were landing under your center of gravity because you didn't wanna slip and fall. If you would have had an overstride, had poor form or been outside your center of gravity, you would have fell down. In Minnesota, I sometimes have clients purposely run on ice in the middle of winter (yes, I know, I'm a sick man). It serves the same purpose.

Remember to think about those visuals: monitor your cadence, try to be at 88-90 SPM, think about running on eggshells, on the side of the pool or on ice, and really focus on minimizing your impact forces as much as possible. It's going to have a huge effect on the wear and tear on your body and how you feel on a day-to-day training basis.

22. KEY AREAS TO STRETCH

In triathlon, certain muscles are prone to getting tight and constricted, and it can dramatically affect your running form if you don't make a concerted effort to keeping those muscles loose. Two different ways to look at it: Swimming is a shoulder-dominant and back-dominant exercise. That's why good swimmers almost always have broad shoulders – those are the muscles being used. Again, that's all well and good from a tone, aesthetic and muscular definition standpoint, but you also have to understand that if you don't work to keep these muscles loose, it "protracts" you, or pulls you forward, and it can hinder your running stride. Specifically, it will cause you to be in a bent over posture, which will shorten your stride when you run. So, pay attention to keeping your back and shoulder muscles loose so you're able to maintain an upright, proud posture with the chest out and shoulder blades back.

The second part to focus on is tightness associated with cycling. Obviously, cycling is a leg-dominant exercise and you're going to be using a lot of hip flexors and quadriceps. Both of the muscles are on the front of the legs and they need to be kept loose as well, for a similar reason to what I described from swimming. When those get tight, it's going to shorten your stride. It will also make you more robotic, unnatural and less economical as you run. Your stride won't be as relaxed and flowing.

If you've gotten done with a hard swim or hard bike ride, and you have a run scheduled for the next day, make sure that you stretch those areas well and you keep them loose because it's going to affect your run stride. The same thing applies if you get off the bike in a race and you feel like your legs are a bit locked up when you're starting the run. You can actually pull off to the side and quickly stretch out those areas.

The last area to pay attention to is your calves. In cycling, I talked about cleat position and how it's going to potentially engage more or less of your calf muscles. You want to keep these muscles loose, not so much because it's going to affect your stride rate or stride length when you're running, but it will definitely affect your propensity for injuries. I've seen a lot of pulled calf muscles, Achilles tendons and planter fasciitis. *Nobody* wants that. The rehab process is long and brutal. All of these tissues are interconnected from the bottom of the foot, all the way up to your knee. Make sure to stretch these areas consistently as well.

23. RELAX YOUR HANDS

The best runners (and the best athletes, in general) do an amazing job of relaxing all the muscles that are not going into propulsion and helping them move forward at a faster rate. Why waste energy otherwise?

The place that all tension starts when you're running is in the hands. In other words, you have to *first* focus on what's going on with your hands, because if your hands aren't loose, your forearms can't be loose, your shoulders can't be loose and your neck can't be loose. It all has to start from your HANDS and then it all flows up from there.

Most people also don't realize that your legs follow your arms in running. I see it happen often (especially in newbie runners), where people will get tired and think about moving their legs faster. You should think of the exact opposite! Think about moving your ARMS faster. If you practice moving your arms faster, your legs will follow. They will naturally follow the pattern, or the rate, in which you swing your arms. You can only swing your arms faster, and at a higher rhythm and cadence, if they're relaxed. You can't do it if you have massive amounts of tension in your hands, forearms and shoulders. You *need* them to be loose and relaxed.

24. TRAIN ON SOFT TERRAIN

We've talked about this already in regards to cadence but the less impact forces you can have on your body, the less susceptible you'll be to running-related injuries. A big component of this is to *train on the softest surface that you possibly can*. It has a massive effect on residual wear and tear.

In order of what's best and what's worse, grass would be the ideal. Trails (whether it's dirt, mulch or gravel) are next best. Tar would be after that, with concrete ranking last. Concrete is the most difficult surface to run on because it's the hardest, and thus, it's going to cause the most impact forces on your body. It's very difficult to stay injury-free and maintain the health of your connective tissue, tendons and ligaments if you're doing all of your training on concrete.

If you're a lucky one who lives on the beach, you might be wondering about training on soft sand. This is the opposite end of the extreme and is not ideal either. If the surface is too soft, your muscles will have to work overtime as well. No good. I've done some beach running at high tide when the sand is hard-packed. This is okay and similar to running on grass.

It's the basic principle of getting off concrete and harder surfaces that matters most. You probably won't notice a difference in the first couple of workouts or even in the first week, but if you continue to run on this type of surface over the course of an entire training season, you're going to feel and recover better on a day-to-day training basis.

Preventing Overuse Injuries in Endurance Athletes

Chronic overuse injuries are prevalent among endurance athletes. This videoconference with Dr. Nolan Mitchell gives you essential strategies to proactively prevent injuries instead of react to them.
Prehab is ALWAYS better than rehab!

Free Instant Access at:
OutperformTheNorm.com/books

25. QUALITY OVER QUANTITY

I'll let you in on a little secret – especially if you're a brand new triathlete, almost *any* miles or *any* amount of swimming, biking or running activity that you do will result in positive progress. It's the nice thing about being brand new to the sport. You're getting used to the sports and anything you do (within reason) is going to make you better.

However, there are certain types of workout that will get you better results, faster. The longer you've been in the sport, the more you have to emphasize the quality of your workouts instead of the quantity. By quantity I mean the duration and mileage. You want to maximize the effectiveness of each workout.

OUTPERFORMING TIPS

First, get out of the "gray area" when you're running. The gray area is what I refer to when you're doing workouts that are "kinda hard." The reason this is not good is because usually what happens with doing kinda hard workouts in the gray area is that it's too hard to let your body optimally recover, but it's not hard enough to produce gains that will allow you to get faster. It's the worst of both worlds.

What you want to do is consciously be thinking about separating hard and easy. THAT is how the most successful triathletes get faster. They either go really easy, where they're developing their aerobic system and their body's ability to burn fat, or they're going really hard, which builds their ability to tolerate lactic acid and makes them faster. Separating these two types of workouts is how to maximize the effectiveness and the quality of your workouts.

The second part is to know what you're working on. When you go for a given run, you should know what desired effect you're seeking from that workout. In other words, ask yourself, "what benefits is this workout going to produce?" When you're doing hill runs, it's going to produce greater benefits in stride length. When you're doing speed work, it's going to produce greater benefits in stride rate. When you're doing intervals, it's going to produce greater benefits in running economy.

One thing on speed work – most people *think* they're doing speed work when they run anything that's roughly a mile or shorter. That's not speed work. What I'm talking about with speed work is really short, really fast strides. Intervals that are less than 45 seconds in duration. It's something that will allow your legs to move faster and will produce great benefits in stride rate. Anything longer than 45 seconds puts lactic acid into the body and actually *counteracts* speed.

The last part of emphasizing quality is improving your running economy. This is what I refer to as lactate tolerance (what many people refer to as speed work) and it's comprised of intervals from 1 minute, all the way up to 12-15 minutes. And, to make sure we're clear, if you've never heard the term lactic acid, it's what makes your muscles burn, ache and get tired when you're doing very challenging workouts. These workouts help with running economy, or how "economical" you are when you run (think miles-per-gallon for your car). It helps you to maintain good running form and to maintain a good pace as your body gets fatigued.

That's how you emphasize quality over quantity. These things are critically important. Get out of the gray area and separate hard and easy. Do more hills if you want longer strides. Do more speed work with short, fast intervals if you want greater stride rate. And do more, longer intervals to increase your running economy and your ability to resist fatigue. When you do this, you know you're making every workout count.

26. DO BRICK RUNS

If you don't know what a "brick run" actually is, it's a run that is done *immediately* after you're done with a bike (to simulate what will happen in a triathlon). I have no idea why they call it a brick run. It's a triathlon term, but it's critically important that you do brick runs because running, and running *after you have just biked*, are two totally different things. You can barely even relate the two, as far as how your legs feel. I've seen a lot of people that are actually pretty good runners, but then they try to run *after* they've biked let's say 10, 25, 56, or 112 miles and they don't even look like the same person. They have a different level of fatigue in their legs. Their quadriceps and hip flexors are tight, and their stride ends up looking unnatural and choppy. It's a much different breed of animal than normal running.

Whether you're new to the sport or experienced, it's a key, critical component to practice doing brick runs in training. What you want to think of when you're doing brick runs is to have practice conditions mirror performance conditions (here we go again). You want to minimize the amount of time that you take from when you finish your bike to when you start your run. You don't want to wait 15 or 20 minutes before you go out for your run because that's not going to replicate when will happen in a race, where you finish the bike and a minute or two later, you're starting your run.

To mimic racing as much as possible, have your running shoes set out ahead of time, so when you finish your bike, you can immediate take off your cycling shoes, put on your running shoes and bolt out the door.

Ideally, you'll be doing at least one brick run per week. That's what I have almost all of my clients do, so you stay used to what it feels like to run *after* you've gotten done biking. It doesn't have to be a hard or a long bike. It's something that you want to get used to not only from mental standpoint, but also from a physical standpoint. Doing consistent brick runs will build your confidence and when race day comes, you'll be prepared and know what to expect.

27. PROPER PACING

Most triathletes (and runners, in general) pace themselves horribly. Sorry, it's true. They start out too fast, waste too much energy and run out of gas towards the end of the race. This ruins all the time they've invested in training. They crash and burn.

To pace yourself properly, start out slooowly and run negative splits. Negative splits mean that if you were to take a given run of any distance and separate it into two equal halves, the second half would be faster than the first half. This is important, not only from a mental perspective, in knowing that you can push through adversity, but also from a physical perspective, in teaching your body to resist fatigue and to continue getting faster as it gets tired.

I'm not saying you're going to be faster in the second half of the run in every triathlon you do. Especially in longer races, there's a residual fatigue that builds up and it's probably inevitable that you're going to slow down a little bit. But it's the *thought process* of trying to get faster over time that you should be focusing on. In fact, for every minute you gain early in a race where you're going faster than you should be, you'll give back 2-3 minutes later in the race. REMEMBER. THIS. STATISTIC. You want to be thinking about settling into your running stride, starting out slowly, finding your rhythm and then picking it up from there. You'll cross the finish line with a smile on your face but it is something you have to simulate in training so that when you get out there and it matters most, you're able to deliver.

3 Essential Elements to
RACING YOUR BEST

Racing your best requires 3 essential elements.
The video is included here because one of the keys is proper pacing, which is a vastly overlooked aspect of endurance sports. If you want to know the other elements, please watch the video.

Free Instant Access at:
OutperformTheNorm.com/books

28. EQUALIZE YOUR EFFORT

Triathlon is about more than fitness – it's also about skill and strategy, both in training and racing. You want to maximize your efficiency when you're out there on the course. This is something that I see runners do wrong all the time and I challenge you to pay attention to it. Next time you're doing any type of race, or if you're on a training run, watch the people with whom you're running. What you're going to find is they almost all go too hard on the uphills. You can hear them wasting energy by their breathing as they're going uphill. Then, when they get to a downhill, you're going to see them leaning back and not taking the free speed. In fact, they barely run any faster on the downhill than they necessarily would have on a flat. It's very similar to cycling, where you crest a hill and don't continue pedaling and pushing the gear on the downhill on the bike, because you're too tired from going up.

Best way is it to equalize your effort, which means going a little bit easier on the uphills (assuming it's not the type of workout where you're *supposed to* go hard on the uphills). If you've got a *really* steep uphill on a training run or race, it's fine to WALK that uphill. In Ironman Wisconsin, they have a couple of steep hills on the run course and even the professional triathletes will walk those uphills. They know it's going to be a significant energy waster, relative to the amount of time they would actually save from running the hills.

By conserving energy on the uphills, you also get to take advantage of the flip side, which is to take the speed on the downhills. Again, most people lean back and put on the brakes when they're going downhill. What you actually want to think of when you have subtle grades and downhills is to lean slightly forward and spin your legs underneath you. DO NOT put on the brakes. You've got the free speed from going downhill, you may as well take it. It makes no sense to hold back, which, truthfully, is going to result in *greater* impact forces and be *harder* on your body. Plus, you're not going any *faster*. It's a triple whammy...and not in a good way.

Focus on taking the free speed on the downhills, equalizing your effort and not going too hard on the uphills. I guarantee it's going to help you have more energy, especially later in your training runs and races.

29. DO STRIDES

Strides are one of the most critical parts of your running program and not a lot of people do them. I have all of my clients do strides almost every week and it has a massive impact on their running. From a time investment perspective, there's no better ROI for your running performance than strides.

Strides are "controlled" sprints. You're not going out there and sprinting like you did when you were in junior high or high school. That's the quickest way to tear a hamstring. Strides are done at about 80 to 90 percent effort of how fast you could run if you were going all out, and they're very short in distance and duration. They're not any farther than probably 100-120 yards, maximum, and are not any longer than 20-30 seconds. They build *neuromuscular speed*. If I were to snap my fingers, that's the type of speed that you ultimately get from doing strides. You get that snappy, fast POP in your legs that a lot of us lose as we age. We get used to running at the same speed (similar to cycling). Similar to the way EHIs break up the rhythm when you are cycling, strides break up the monotony and rhythm of always running at the same pace too.

Add these into your program at least once a week, and do anywhere from 4-10 strides. Focus on 80-90% percent effort and on nothing else other than moving your legs *faster than they normally move*. It only takes 20-30 seconds and you will notice a distinct difference in your stride rate. When you do these strides over time, they will start to naturally blend into your regular running stride, where you'll find it's easier for you to run with a higher cadence (88-90). Continue to stack 'em week after week, month after month, and I promise you, you will notice a substantial improvement in your running times.

30. THE BIG THREE WORKOUTS

If you want to run your absolute best, it centers around three key workouts every single week. Doing additional runs above and beyond these is fine, but it's gravy on the mashed potatoes.

The 3 key workouts that every runner needs to be doing if they want to improve are one quality speed workout, one quality hill workout and one quality long run. The type of race (and the course terrain) will dictate exactly how you *execute* these workouts, but if you focus on nothing else other than these, it's going to help your running because it will be focused and targeted. You'll have a nice blend of strides for neuromuscular speed with intervals for running economy and your ability to resist fatigue. This comes from your quality speed workout. Your quality hill run will help with stride length and your ability to build a powerful push off. Your quality long run will build your connective tissues, acclimate you to a longer time on your feet, and teach your body to utilize fat as a fuel source.

For these 3 key workouts, you want to have at least 48 hours in between each workout. For example, most of my clients will do their speed work and interval work on Tuesdays, on Thursdays they'll do their hill work, and then on either Saturday/Sunday, they'll do their long run. It's not to say that they won't have a couple other shorter runs, but any of these runs are done *very easily* throughout the course of the week (remember, stay out of the gray area!). They're probably 20-45 minutes, and they're meant to clear out the lactic acid. It's Tuesday, Thursday, Saturday/Sunday that are their big 3 workouts throughout the week.

If you focus on *really* doing these 3 workouts well, you'll continue to improve, regardless of whether you're a new or experienced triathlete.

SECTION 4
MINDSET

"Your mind is your greatest asset
or your largest liability."

31. OWN THE COMMITMENT

Triathlon is a huge time commitment and the longer the race you're doing, the greater the commitment required. I often tell my clients when they're looking at potentially signing up for a race that if you're going to do a race, and *especially* a longer distance race (say a 70.3 or an Ironman), you have to be ready to take on a part time job. That's the volume of training required at your maximum durations.

Along with this, it's not only a time commitment that you're spending swimming, biking and running, but it's also the *energy* commitment that goes into it as well. If you do a 100-mile bike ride on a Saturday morning, or a 20-mile run on a Sunday, you're not going to have nearly as much energy after that as you would on a normal Saturday or Sunday (makes sense, right?). You want to make sure you own this commitment from day one or it's going to be a rude awakening.

If you have a family and/or if you have kids, you want to make sure that they're on board. I'm obviously not trying to talk you out of anything because, more than anyone else, I firmly believe that it's worth it in the long run. Everything worthwhile in life requires commitment and hard work. But I've seen people watch someone else train, race and accomplish a goal. Then, they decide, 'Oh yes, I'm going to do this thing,' without really realizing and recognizing how much goes into it, from a time and energy standpoint.

Make sure you cover your bases, not only for yourself, but also for your family and friends. *Own that commitment* from day one. You'll be tired and the hours can get long, but remember, the accomplishment *will be* worth it.

32. REMOVE SELF-IMPOSED LIMITATIONS

Self-imposed limitations are things we have in our heads about how we conceptualize our own potential and what we're capable of accomplishing. It's the governor on what we feel we can do. We can look at it from a lot of different levels, not only with triathlon, but many of us have the same self-imposed limitations professionally...or even if we're looking for a dating partner. We have an amount we feel we're worth and a level of attractiveness we think we deserve. This could be another book by itself, but these self-imposed limitations flow into every single aspect of our lives.

I see it a lot with clients and in triathlon. For example, let's take running. Early on when I'm working with a new client, I will tell them what "splits" I want them to run at the track (in speed work). In other words, how fast I want them to run, for a 400 or an 800 or a mile. And it's almost always *faster* than they're used to running (remember the *Gray Area* tip?). They'll look at me with this deer-in-headlights look and say, "Scott, I don't think I can run that fast."

I would obviously never ask a client to do something that I didn't honestly believe they were capable of doing, and that look they give me is, 100%, their own self-imposed limitations. They simply don't believe that they're *capable* of running any faster (or swimming/biking any faster).

I used to see it when I was doing personal training and I would give a client a heavier weight than they were used to lifting. They didn't think they were able to lift the weight initially, but inevitably, every single person I've ever asked to lift a given weight has ended up being able to do it. Sometimes, it takes someone else telling you, "Hey, you really can do this! You don't have to have these self-imposed limitations on yourself!"

Now, I'm obviously never going to be able to bike like Lance Armstrong, swim like Michael Phelps or run like a Kenyan, but we all have governors in the form of self-imposed limitations and our own capabilities. I will challenge you as we go through this *Mindset* section that whatever you think your self-imposed limitations are, actively try to remove them as soon as possible. Once you are able to do that, your true potential comes out as a triathlete.

33. SET PERFORMANCE GOALS

There are three types of goals you can set: *Performance Goals*, *Process Goals* and *Outcome Goals*. I'll start with Outcome Goals because that's where a lot of people put their stock and it's the type of goal many people set.

Outcome Goals are based on how you finish relative to someone else in a given competition or a given race. So, for example, I placed 10th in my age group. Or I was the 16th female that crossed the finish line. This type of goal is all well and good but is this the type of goal that you *really* want to set? If you finished 10th in your age group, do you have any control over how the top 9 people finished? The answer is NO. If you're the person that finished 16th, do you have any control over the top 15 people? NO.

All you can do is execute *your own personal best performance*, and this is done through performance goals.

Performance Goals are based on your own previous standards and benchmarks you've set. It's you against you. You're trying to improve against yourself. They're the best types of goals you can set. You could go out, finish 10th and have your best race ever. But if the top 9 people all have their best race ever and you're basing all of your worth on outcome goals, it's not going to work out. You're judging yourself based on what other people are doing.

Contrast this with focusing on how you can improve your own individual performance and have your best race ever. That's something where you can go home, look yourself in the mirror and feel good about what you've done because you've based your goals on your own personal standards.

The third type of goal is *Process Goals*. Process goals are given movements or patterns that ultimately go into the *execution* of a given activity. So, for something like cycling, it would be focussing on getting the body weight on the pedals, swimming would be getting a feel for the water and calmly breathing. Running would be pulling from the hamstrings and staying relaxed. Those are a few different examples, but process goals are going to allow you to execute a given performance better. I try to individualize process goals for my clients so they can get the most out of every training session or race.

Start out with performance goals and focusing on improving against your own previous standards. It will facilitate not only

OUTPERFORM THE NORM

your motivation, but also your mindset and desire to train and race.

Time Trialing and Performance Improvements

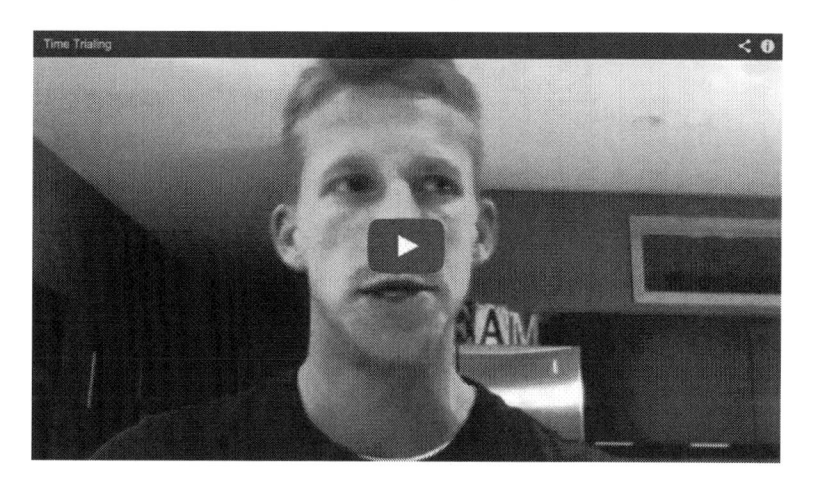

I have many of my clients do periodic "time trials," which measures your individual progress against your personal best. Watch this video to find out why it's the single best strategy to build motivation and improve your performance.

Free Instant Access at:
OutperformTheNorm.com/books

34. MUSTERING MOTIVATION

Triathlon training can be difficult. Seasons can get long and you'll be tired. Sometimes, I affectionately refer to this tiredness as "walking death." You're not only mentally tired but you're physically tired, then you look at your calendar and you know you have to get on your bike, jump in the pool or go for a run and you don't feel like doing it. The motivation is simply not there.

Put bluntly, you have to determine whether your body has been pushed past its acceptable limits or whether you're lazy and mentally not up for the workout. To answer this question, I always encourage my clients to simply commit to the warm up. You have to ascertain whether your lack of motivation is physical or whether it's mental. If it's mental, you can push through that. You push through it by committing to the warm up. It can be a matter of getting *started* and shaking out the cobwebs.

But if you get out there and, after the first 10-15 minutes, you still feel dead tired, that's fine. You turn around and head back home. It's okay. Usually this means your body is telling you something and you need to listen to it, which feeds into the next point regarding overtraining...

35. MONITOR YOUR MOOD

Monitoring your mood is a strong indicator of overtraining and it's probably the best one you have, speaking from personal experience. One of the best ways that I can monitor whether I'm overtraining (or under-recovering) is if I'm sitting around in the middle of a Minnesota summer and it's an absolutely gorgeous day with bright sunshine, and there's nothing that I would rather do than *lay on the couch*. There's no part of me that wants to go outside. I would rather watch TV than hang with Mother Nature.

I know when I have that feeling that something is wrong. I'm either overtrained or under-recovered (I use the terms synonymously). I probably need to step things back, get more sleep, be nicer to my body and possibly skip a work out or two. There are many indications (from a mood standpoint) for overtraining that you need to pay attention to. Some of these are:

- ✓ Feeling lethargic
- ✓ Depression
- ✓ Decreased appetite
- ✓ Decreased sex drive
- ✓ Poor quality of sleep
- ✓ Apathy

Triathlon is great, but these feelings affect everything in life (relationships, productivity, etc.). Probably not worth it.

Especially if you're new to triathlon, you're not going to know what I'm talking about until you get into the thick of training. Then you'll understand what I mean. But it's something that you have to pay attention to. Not only how your body is physically feeling as far as aches and pains, but also drastic changes in your attitude and mood. They're a big indicator of whether you need to step it back and give your body more time to recover on a day-to-day basis. Ignore these signs and you can end up reeking havoc on your hormones (and the glands that produce them), and your chances for injury. Tread lightly.

36. EXPECT THE BEST - PREPARE FOR THE WORST

I always tell all my clients when we have pre-race meetings that, regardless of what distance a race they're training for, to *expect the best but prepare for the worst*. Don't get me wrong, I absolutely WANT their race (and all of your races!) to go perfectly start to finish. I want them to have no issues, to have the time of their life and their best possible performance.

But what I'm telling you to guard against is thinking that nothing can (and will) go wrong. Something *always* happens that is different from what you'd expect. This happens to professional triathletes who have done hundreds of races. It keeps thing interesting. Never a dull moment.

If you've heard my own personal story, you'd know that Ironman was the first triathlon I ever *completed*. But it wasn't supposed to be that way. I signed up for the Chisago Lakes Half

Ironman a month and half before Ironman Wisconsin. In that race, the swim went ok and the bike was going along fine too, until mile 42, where I got a flat tire. I got off, changed it, and rode about another mile up the road. Flatted again. Changed it, got on the bike, and didn't make it more than a half mile up the road before I got *another* flat.

My race was over.

It turned out there was a piece of glass that was stuck in between my tire and my rim that caused me to keep getting these flats. At the time, I was absolutely devastated (it was my first triathlon!). I went out there naively thinking that everything would go *perfectly* start to finish. I didn't ever stop to think that it is possible for things to not work out. I didn't factor in that shit happens.

I wish none of this on you, but I do want you to be prepared that if adversity happens, you're able to respond to it. It doesn't have to be in the form of you dropping out of a race because you get a flat tire (that's the worst case scenario, other than an injury or accident). I'm talking about simple things like your goggles getting knocked off on the swim, or a shoelace breaks on the run, or your race belt doesn't work. These are all things that have actually happened to me before. Responding to them and not getting rattled is what counts.

37. KNOW YOUR PURPOSE

Why are you doing triathlon? Seriously. Why are you doing it? What is your purpose and why are you reading this right now? I know that may seem like a deep question but hopefully you have the answer. If you haven't thought about it, now is a good time to start.

Everybody has a different reason for doing triathlon. Maybe you've recovered from some physical ailment and you want to go out there and use your newfound zest for life. Maybe you want to be a role model and set a good example for your kids. Maybe there's somebody that you're competing against that you desperately want to beat. Maybe you want to prove someone else wrong. Maybe you have a background in the sport and you want to continue to get better and improve your triathlon skills.

Everybody has their own individual purpose but you need to KNOW yours.

You need to know your purpose because it's what you come back to when the going gets tough out on the race course. And it WILL. It always does, regardless of whether you're doing a sprint distance triathlon or an Ironman. You're going to get to certain spots on the swim, bike and *certainly* on the run where the going gets TOUGH. I always tell people, if you don't bring it to the race, you're not going to find it out there.

That's why I'm bringing this up now. You have to know why you're putting yourself out there. Why you do triathlon and why you're reading this right now. Then you want to come back to it when the going gets tough. It will mentally fuel your motivation when every single thing in your body is screaming at you to walk, stop or quit and to not go any further. Your purpose keeps you moving forward and is a distinguishing characteristic of the mentally toughest triathletes.

38. MAKE THE MOST OF YOUR POTENTIAL

I'm going to start out by telling you a story of a client that I had a couple of years ago. Very high-level athlete. She qualified for the Half Ironman World Championships. I coached her to 3:17:00 finish at the Chicago marathon and she had completed her best racing season ever.

The Chicago marathon takes place in October. She went out to Colorado three months later in January to go skiing, and I'm not talking about the bunny hill – she was doing moguls and double black diamonds. Unfortunately, she tore her ACL and had surgery, but there was a glitch in the surgery. She ended up with a staph infection because of complications from the procedure. She needed to have another surgery. But there were more problems. She's never been the same since.

Doctors have told her that she'll probably never run again. She has too much pain in her knee. It's a tragic story because you realize how quickly some of these things can be stripped away from you. She ran that 3:17 at Chicago in October, then three months later she tears her ACL and her competitive running career is over. She's trying to get back at it now and she runs with a brace on. But when she runs, she has severe swelling and she's never going to be able to do the things that she used to be able to do. Very sad.

Take home point – make the most of your potential. You never know when something unforeseen can happen and it can be taken away from you.

I have no idea why you've come to this book. You may be doing your first triathlon or you may be trying to qualify for

Kona. Whichever one it is, go out there and give it everything you've got! Give it your heart. Give it your soul. Try your best. Make the most of the gifts you've been given because you don't know when they may go. These are good lessons for all of us to remember.

Soak it up...in triathlon and in life.

SECTION 5
PERFORMANCE NUTRITION

"Fuel up. Keep up. Recover.
That is how you Outperform."

39. ART AND SCIENCE

I always say there's both art and science to performance nutrition. Yes, there have been phenomenal advances and research done in the last few years in terms of how our body *responds* to intense exercise, how our body *recovers* from exercise and how to *fuel* our body optimally for performance. Despite this science, we're still on the forefront of putting it all together. We certainly have a better understanding of it now than we used to...even though there is still a lot to uncover.

Even with these scientific advances, there is a large component of performance nutrition that I call *art*. Everybody's body is very different. I think of all the athletes that I've ever worked with and coached. I can take two athletes of similar builds, body types, heights and weights and give them the exact same formulation (scientifically speaking) of products. One will perform phenomenally well and the other will have digestive issues and barely be able to finish. Crazy, but not that far from the truth. Behold the principle of *individual differences*.

That's the "art" side of things where you never know how an athlete is going to *respond* to taking in certain foods, whether it's fluids or solids during training or a competition. This is where trial and error comes into play. You have to practice what you're going to do when it matters most. Practice conditions *have to* mirror performance conditions.

That's where performance nutrition starts – you must appreciate and understand everybody's body is unique. So is yours. I will certainly make recommendations based on science and what I've seen with my own clients, as far as what to have beforehand, during and after, as well as hydration and electrolyte replacement. All these things are great but you *still* have to find out what works best for YOU. The only way that is going to happen is if you do a little bit of practicing and tinkering and tweaking to find out how your body best responds to performance nutrition.

40. THE FOUNDATIONAL LAYER

The best way to explain performance nutrition and nutritional supplementation is to look at it like a house. If you want your house to be sturdy, durable and to stand the test of time, it needs to have a strong foundation. It needs to be built to last.

There are three crucial products that I refer to as the *foundational layer*:

- ✓ Multivitamin
- ✓ Fish oil
- ✓ Probiotic

The reason this foundational layer is so important is, regardless of whether you're a professional level or elite level triathlete, or whether you're someone that's getting into the sport, triathlon is a game of energy (yes, I know I've said that before!). You want your energy in triathlon to be specifically geared towards helping you recover, repair and rebuild from your training and racing.

The only way you can do that is if you're giving it the appropriate nutritional supplementation (in addition to food).

our energy going towards repairing and rebuilding, bolstering your immune system and fighting off ., or fighting off weird aches and pains because of inadequate nutrition and dietary deficiencies. That's where the foundational layer comes in and why these three products are important.

To quickly go into the details of each, the multivitamin fills in the gaps in your nutritional holes. No one gets all of the vitamins and minerals and nutrients that they need through food right now. It can't happen. The soil quality isn't as good as it once was, foods are stripped of many of their vital nutrients through manufacturing and processing and, unless you have your own personal chef, you're probably not eating all colours of the rainbow every single day, which means you need some type of *quality* multivitamin to fill in your gaps and to help curb your nutritional deficiencies.

The second piece is a good fish oil. Fish oil is important not only for hair and skin and nails, and for heart health and brain health. It's also important for lubrication of the joints, which is crucial in triathlon because it's a game of dehydration and rehydration as you're training a lot, especially outdoors. You want to make sure that you have good fats coming into your body through fish oils. If you have a history of cardiovascular disease, or a family history of dementia, fish oils become even more necessary. It's a product that every person should be on.

The third product is a probiotic. A probiotic puts the good bacteria into your digestive system. It's key because the majority of your immune system resides in your stomach and your digestive tract. Most people don't realize that there are good bacteria and bad bacteria, and you need to put the good bacteria into your body to help do away with some of the bad bacteria. To come back to where I started, you want to do this because you don't want your body to be expending energy trying to fight off sickness and infections. You want your energy going towards helping your body perform its best.

My personal favourite brand is **AdvoCare nutrition products**. Yes, I am involved with the company but I use their products religiously and I passionately believe they are one of the best in the industry. There are other quality companies out there but AdvoCare is what I recommend to all of my clients. Build that foundational layer and you will see your performance (and health) dramatically improve over time.

41. GETTING LEAN AND MEAN

Eating for a lean body composition is what all triathletes are after and there's a specific method of eating that facilitates this result. It's counter intuitive and definitely different than the way a lot of people eat on a day-to-day basis. The way the majority of people eat is to have three squares a day of breakfast, lunch and dinner.

To eat for a lean body composition and to fuel your metabolism, however, you need to be a grazer and not a binger. By "grazing," I mean eating small amounts, frequently throughout the course of the day.

So, you're still having your three squares, with breakfast, lunch and dinner. But sprinkled in between those meals, you're also having a mid-morning snack and a mid-afternoon snack. Included in those snacks of mid morning and mid afternoon is protein, because it's the building block of muscle. It is necessary for tone and definition and what your body needs to have the shape and the tone that you desire. It's critically important to have protein at both of these meals.

Ideally, you would be eating about every three hours. This means breakfast, mid-morning snack, lunch, mid-afternoon snack and dinner. This is your *general* meal plan. I understand if you're training for a longer distance triathlon that there are some days you could be on the bike for five or six hours. On these days, it might not be feasible to eat that many times. But, in general, to fuel a lean body composition, it is imperative to have small amounts, frequently and have protein sprinkled into each of these meals.

Protein is going to keep your metabolism burning strong. It doesn't have to be a lot, about 10-25 grams of protein at each meal is plenty. You don't want to go above 25 grams because your body can't metabolize all the protein and it will inevitably convert some of it to stored body fat. By hitting these amounts, you're going to be lean and mean and have the body composition that you desire.

42. NO LOW CARB DIETS

A few years ago the low carb (or no carb) diets swept the country as a way that people could lose weight and decrease body fat. I've even seen it make its way into endurance sports. It's the furthest thing from what you want to do in your diet when you are training for a triathlon. The specific reason is that your body burns carbohydrates for fuel. THAT is what it needs and if you don't give it what it needs, it's not going to be able to perform.

Studies have shown that in endurance exercise of roughly 2-2.5 hours, your body uses almost completely stored body fat or carbohydrates for fuel (depending on intensity). Beyond 2-2.5 hours, it's still only going to use roughly 8-10% of protein as a fuel source and the rest is going to be stored body fat or carbohydrate. Sometimes, I still see people wanting to take in higher amounts of protein while they're working out, even when they're doing a really long training bike or swim or run. It doesn't make any sense. It's NOT what your body is using for fuel.

Think about it outside of exercise as well. The stored form of carbohydrate in the body is called *glycogen* and your body can store roughly 90 minutes of muscle glycogen during endurance exercise at any given time. Outside of what you actually take in *during* exercise, you need to make sure your glycogen stores are topped off before you go into training or racing.

Look at it like the gas tank on your car. If you're not replenishing what your body is burning during exercise then you're starting your car, or going into your next training session, with less than a full tank. The ideal is that you're always going to starting with a full gas tank because that's how you're going to perform your best.

Stay away from any type of low carb diet if you're training for a triathlon. Your body and brain and performance and recovery will thank you for it.

43. FUEL UP AND KEEP UP

The specific nutritional strategy that I use with clients is called *Fuel Up, Keep Up, Recover*. I'll deal with the *Recover* side of things later, but first we'll go over the *Fuel Up* and *Keep Up* parts of it because they are absolutely essential to your performance.

Fuel Up is making sure that you give your body what it needs pre-training (or pre-competition) to be at its best. From a food choice standpoint, you want to be taking in something that's high in carbohydrates, moderate/low in protein and low in fat. I would add something that's low in fiber as well, and especially if you're running. If you take in too much fiber before running, trust me, it's not going to be a "pleasant" experience :)

In terms of calories, you want to look at roughly 200-300 calories for every hour pre-work out or pre-competition that you are eating. In other words, if you're eating one hour before a workout, you want something that's about 200-300 calories.

If you're eating two hours before a workout, you'd want to take in something that's 400-600 calories. The maximum duration I would ever recommend would be three hours before a workout. 600-900 calories, for many people, is a ton of food. That's why the sweet spot for you would be somewhere around the two hour mark. Again, follow the parameters of high in carbohydrate, moderate/low in protein and low in fat for fuel choices. This will ascertain that the food will be digested more fully and absorbed into your system when you go out on your swim, bike or run.

These are examples of good carbohydrate fuel choices:

- ✓ Wholegrain Oatmeal
- ✓ Steel Cut Oats
- ✓ Muesli
- ✓ Brown Rice
- ✓ Quinoa
- ✓ Sweet Potatoes
- ✓ Baked Potatoes

For protein:

- ✓ Greek Yogurt or regular yogurt
- ✓ Eggs
- ✓ Milk (if dairy agrees with you)
- ✓ Peanut Butter or other nut butters

Most of these choices will also give you some fat as well.

For *Keep Up*, you want to target roughly 200-400 calories per hour, depending on your body weight. If you're a slighter female (ballpark weight of 120-130lbs), you'd probably be closer to 200-250 calories per hour. For me, weighing in at 185lbs, with reasonably dense muscle on my frame, I target 400 calories per hour.

This is something that you want to take in every single hour that you're out there. What it's going to do is keep your fuel tanks as full as possible while you're exercising and make sure you don't hit the dreaded "wall" and don't bonk when you're out there. There's nothing worse than running out of gas when you're on the course. Specifically, I'm talking about doing these things during training so they will carry over to what you're doing during racing. Remember – practice conditions mirror performance conditions!

Your core requirements for 200-400 calories an hour can come in the form of what you drink OR what you eat, but it's going to be something that's almost straight carbohydrates. It needs to be something that gets into your system very fast and also slowly drips into the system. They call this "sequential carbs." A lot of gels now have sequential carbohydrates. It means you'll have some carbohydrates that get into your system quickly, some that are released moderately and some that take a little longer to get into your system.

To go back to the "art" part of performance nutrition, if you focus on meeting these caloric requirements (200-400 per hour) AND have some blend of sequential carbohydrates, you'll know that you're *Keeping Up* and fuelling your body to perform its best. Most of these calories are going to come from nutrition-specific companies (AdvoCare, Accelerade, Hammer, Endurox, etc.) and you will have to use trial and error to find out what works best for you.

44. HYDRATION AND ELECTROLYTES

Hydration is key to helping you perform your best. Obviously, if you're training for a triathlon you're probably somewhere in a warm whether climate where you're going to be sweating a lot. Studies show that for every 1-2% of your body weight that you lose through dehydration, it will have a corresponding 2-3% decrease on your performance.

Hydration is a BIG deal.

Think about it from my standpoint again – if I'm weighing in at 185 lbs and I lose roughly 1.85 lbs through sweat (which is 1% of my body weight), that's going to have a corresponding 2-3% decrease on my performance. This is *really* easy to do, especially if it's hot outside and if there's any level of humidity. It affects every single thing in your body when you're dehydrated. Your physiological functioning and the way your muscles contract, how quickly nutrients are transported through the body and your level of mental and cognitive functioning. Do whatever you can to not let it happen.

For overall daily hydration, you want to make sure that you're taking in a minimum of half of your body weight in ounces of water each day. So, say that I weigh 200 lbs. I would be taking in 100 ounces of water each day. If you weigh 130 lbs, you would be taking in 65 ounces of water each day. That is the *minimum*. This *doesn't* factor in what you are drinking while you are training. This is strictly water and fluids that you take in aside from what you're ingesting during exercise.

One more thing – any diuretics that you take in (alcohol, caffeine, soda, diet soda, energy drinks, coffee, tea) will pull water out of the body, which means you actually have to take in even *more* water if you want to stay optimally hydrated.

The best thing you can do to be sure you're maintaining optimal hydration is to simply weigh yourself before you go out for your training or competition and weigh yourself afterwards. Let's say I go out for a bike ride and I weigh 185 lbs when I start and 182 lbs when I get back, and I know that I took in three bottles of fluid when I was on the bike. I now know that I need to take in an additional 48 ounces of water because I'm losing too high a percentage of my body weight while I'm out there. It's also important to note that the intensity is going to be even higher when I'm racing, which means I'm going to be sweating MORE and I'll need to take in even more additional fluid. This is the best way to determine your own individual sweat rates.

The second part is electrolyte replacement. Obviously, when you're not training you're probably going to be taking in almost plain water exclusively. But while you're working out or competing, you need to be taking in not regular water – you also need to be taking in something to replace the electrolytes you are losing through sweat.

There are four basic electrolytes that you lose when you sweat: calcium, magnesium, potassium and sodium. Ideally what you're going to look for is some type of solution, in a pill form, salt stick or powder that you would put in your bottles while you're biking and running (if you wear a fuel belt). You want something that has a mix of these four electrolytes.

Choosing something that has calcium, magnesium, potassium and sodium gives the product a complete electrolyte profile and will keep you on a more even keel while you're training and competing. It's going to minimize the chance that you'll have any heat-related performance decrements. It's going to minimize the likelihood that you'll have heat exhaustion, cramps, dizziness or nausea.

A lot of mainstream products will layer on the sodium and potassium and neglect magnesium and calcium. The magnesium and calcium are key for cognitive functioning because you have to be mentally alert when you're training, as well as physically alert.

Again, I love AdvoCare products, particularly Rehydrate (their electrolyte replacement). It's what I recommend for people to take in during their training sessions and competitions because it has this complete electrolyte profile in powder or in the gel form. You can find other companies that have similar products, but again, make sure you hit all of those electrolytes and you're not having straight water. You're not losing water through sweat and as long as you layer in these four electrolytes, you'll know you're replacing what you're losing during training or racing.

4 Keys to Beat the Heat in Training & Racing

Triathlon takes place in the summer months. Summer months are hot. When it's hot, you better hydrate and replace your electrolytes or you'll crash and burn.
Watch this video to do it the right way.

Free Instant Access at:
OutperformTheNorm.com/books

45. RECOVER TO BUILD UP

I tell all my athletes that you train to break down; you recover to build up. The recovery part is overlooked by a lot of triathletes and it's a crucial aspect to being able to perform your best. A lot of people don't look at it this way. They think they get stronger during training and racing. And they don't.

What you're doing is breaking your body down, then if you give it what it needs, it will adapt and build up stronger than it was before. Then the next training session comes along and you break your body down again, give it what it needs to build up stronger. This process repeats itself.

The way that you know you're doing this right is that throughout the course of your training season, you should be getting stronger each week and each month. If you're doing this wrong, your body will be getting worse as time goes on. That's obviously not at all what you want and you're going to see it not only physically, but also mentally.

You want to pay attention to what you're doing immediately *after* training. We call it a "glycogen window." I talked about how glycogen is the body's stored form of carbohydrate (or sugar). When you finish a training session, you've got about a 30-minute window where your muscles are like a sponge. They want to soak something up and you have to give them something to soak up within the first 30 minutes of that glycogen window. Take too long and you'll miss this precious time.

The interesting thing is, if you miss this 30-minute window, you probably won't even notice it the next day – you'll notice it the day after, or two days after. You'll go out there for a workout and you'll feel super tired...and you won't know why. Your legs will be heavy and you'll feel like a bus has hit you.

This can almost always be directly traced back to a time where you've missed the 30-minute glycogen window. You didn't give your muscles what they needed when they were like a sponge and wanted to soak something up.

Within 30 minutes of training (or racing), you want to look for something that has roughly a 3:1 or 4:1 ratio of carbohydrates to protein. You want to replace what you burned. Almost all research coming out nowadays says this is the optimal ratio to facilitate your body repairing, rebuilding and recovering from intense exercise. Do this and you're going to notice a huge difference in your ability to get back after it, the next day, after you've had a hard training session.

PERFORMANCE NUTRITION

Heart Rate Training & the Physiology of Recovery

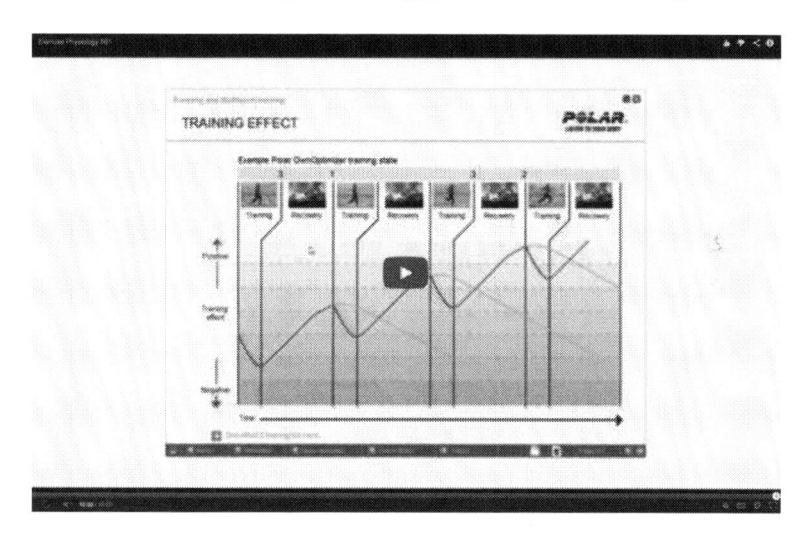

I recorded this video for some of my private coaching clients so they could understand training intensity and the physiology of recovery. If you want to know what's going on inside of your body as you build fitness, this is the video for you.

Instant Access at:
OutperformTheNorm.com/books

SECTION 6
THE FINISH LINE

"In life—and in triathlon—the little things become the big things."

46. THE IMPORTANCE OF SLEEP

The importance of sleep is critical, not only for your general health and wellbeing but also for your triathlon performance. We live in an over-caffeinated, under-rested society. We get by on energy drinks, sodas and diet sodas, caffeinated teas and coffee. And usually we do this because we don't sleep very well, both in terms of sleep *quantity* and sleep *quality*.

Sleep is the time where your body produces key hormones (we referenced these in performance nutrition). You train to break down and you recover to build up. Your ability to repair and rebuild and recover is the single biggest determinant of how your training is going to go throughout the course of an entire training season. This is facilitated largely by hormones that you produce during sleep (particularly, *growth hormone*).

If you're not getting enough quantity of sleep or if the quality of your sleep is not good, it's going to greatly compromise your ability to be your best when it matters the most.

The best tip I can give you in regards to sleep is to simply try to form a pattern, where you're going to bed at the same time every night. Your routine leading up to when you go to bed should be exactly the same as well. If you normally brush your teeth, take a hot bath, read a book, watch TV, or do *whatever* you normally do to unwind, try to keep that routine consistent. We truly are creatures of habit and routine. The more you can establish whatever pattern works for you, the more you can replicate this over time and the better you're going to sleep at night.

One other thing on sleep – be careful of evening or late night workouts. I understand sometimes, especially if you're training for a longer distance triathlon and you have a demanding job where you're working 40+ hours a week, you have to do runs, bikes or swims that are later in the evening. Doing these workouts affects your ability to sleep, specifically your ability to get into REM sleep (quality, deep sleep) throughout the course of the night.

Ideally, try to modify your schedule so that you're doing your workouts earlier in the day. Then, from a nutrition standpoint, try to minimize the amount of caffeine you're taking in later in the day. Everybody has a different caffeine tolerance but try not to take in caffeine after 6pm. Don't drink alcohol before sleep either. Some people think it helps them fall asleep, but it impairs your ability to get into REM sleep, where the really good stuff and the necessary hormones that are triggered during sleep happens.

47. THE IMPORTANCE OF MASSAGE

I used to always look at massage as a luxury. It was something I'd do after I'd done a really hard work out or a hard race. It was my reward for training/racing hard and getting my butt kicked. I never looked at it as being a vital component to helping my body repair and rebuild and recover.

In the last few years I've changed my tune. I now understand that if you're putting your body through the rigors of swimming, biking and running every single day, for weeks on end, certain muscles are going to get tight and bound up. The *only way* that you're ever going to alleviate those knots and get rid of that tension inside your body is to get a good sports massage.

Finding a good massage therapist is like finding a good hair stylist. When you find one, never let them go. Always hold onto them and continue to go back to that person. But use them when you need to maximize your recovery. It's going to make a big difference in your body's ability to stay loose and to stay biomechanically correct. A lot of times things can get out of alignment when our muscles are tight and we aren't symmetrical from left side to right side, top to bottom and front to back.

Don't overlook the importance of massage because it's a critical factor in performing at your best.

NOTE – never get a deep tissue massage the day or two before a race. It's too close and, especially, if you haven't gotten a deep tissue massage in a while, it's normal to be sore afterwards. The same thing goes for post-race – never get a deep tissue massage within 1-2 days of a hard race.

Usually, I will get a deep tissue massage on a Wednesday for a Saturday or Sunday race. This has worked best for my clients and me. Your timing post-race depends on how tired you are and your overall level of soreness.

48. TRANSITIONS

One of the things that really surprised me once I started working more extensively with triathletes and endurance athletes was how much emphasis and weight they would put on transitions. They'd want to map out their transition plan and spend extensive time practicing their transitions.

Think about it – say you're doing an Olympic distance triathlon, with a projected finishing time of about 3 hours. If you add your T1 (your swim to bike transition) and your T2 (your bike to run transition) it will probably be no more than 3-5 minutes, total.

That's 3-5 minutes out of a 3-hour race. As the durations get longer and you start talking about Half Ironmans and Ironmans, you're still talking about roughly the same 3-5 minutes out of roughly 6 hours (for a Half Ironman) or 12-15 hours (for an Ironman), as estimates.

In the grand scheme of your overall finishing time, the transition time doesn't matter.

The best thing is to focus on the quality of your swimming, biking or running, because that's where you're spending the majority of your time. I cannot believe the number of people who sweat saving *seconds* in their transitions, when you could channel that same level of energy to saving *minutes* in swimming, biking or running. I've seen athletes run out of T1 and try to do a flying jump onto their bike without breaking stride, only to tip over and fall flat on their face. Not the ideal way to start the second leg of your triathlon.

Mastering Your Triathlon Transitions

Yes, triathlon transitions have little relevance in the grand scheme of your overall finishing time, but I did record this video for my clients on how to navigate your transitions **efficiently and effectively.**

Free Instant Access at:
OutperformTheNorm.com/books

49. YOUR TRANSITION PLAN

I know I just got done talking about how, in the grand scheme of things, from a time perspective, transitions don't make much of a difference. But that doesn't mean that I send my triathletes blindly into their first triathlon without any type of plan to execute for their transitions. That would be foolish. I wanted to make sure you understood what *really matters* when it comes to finishing times and triathlon performance.

That being said, the single best thing that you can do when you are setting up your transition area is to have a plan in place and to mentally rehearse (if not physically rehearse it) exactly how you're going to go through your transition area. Usually, transition areas are mapped out by number, where you'll have a specific number on your transition stall that corresponds to your race number. That's where you'll set up your bike and have your running shoes and all your other goodies. There isn't a right or a wrong way to set up your transition area but you want to lay out your transition area in a way that you can mentally rehearse the exact order that you're going to execute your transition. This means your running shoes, race belt, cycling shoes, socks, your hat, sunglasses and everything else, is set up in a way that works for YOU.

So, when you come out of the water and you're running into your transition area, before you actually get on the bike, what is the order that you're going to take off your wetsuit, take off your swim cap, take off your goggles, put on your socks, put on your cycling shoes, put on your helmet and put on your glasses? Have a logical plan to get from point A to point B that's structured as far as 1, 2, 3, 4 and then lay your items out accordingly.

You want to do this not only in your T1, but also how you are going to come into your transition area off of your bike and going to the run as well. What is the order that you're going to be taking off your cycling shoes, changing socks, putting on your running shoes, putting on a hat or a visor or a race belt or a fuel belt or any other nutrition? Set up your transition area so you can have a plan and you can be methodical and purposeful when you're going through your transitions.

That's the last point I will leave you with – when you're going through your transition area, be POISED. You don't want a lolly gagging and you certainly don't want to waste time in your transition area. But you do want to be poised and you do want to move with purpose. I think the only way that you can be poised and the only way that you can move with purpose is if you have a plan and if you know the exact order in which you're going to execute your movements. Doing this is going to build your confidence and your ability to execute when it comes to race day.

50. SOAK IT UP AND PAY IT FORWARD

Here in the US, in the 21st century, we have a health crisis. It's an epidemic. I started out this book by saying triathlon has changed my life and if you're new to triathlon, I hope it will change yours as well. What I hope most is that, if we are ever going to help the health of this great country (and the world), and help people be fitter, live longer, have a higher quality of life, that as you drift into your triathlon journey, you'll not only use these tips and do it the right way, but you'll also invite people onto the race course with you. On the day that you're racing, ask them to come out and support you. Hopefully, they'll soak up the great energy, feel the positive triathlon vibe and be inspired to do it themselves.

I honestly think we can change a significant number of lives through sports like triathlon, by getting people more active. Again, it has every single thing going for it – you've got the social support. You've got the fresh air and Mother Nature. You've got the competition. You've got the variety. You've got the cross training. You've got the body.

It's an unbelievable sport to be around and I've been privileged to be a part of it.

I appreciate you reading this book. I hope that these tips meant something to you and you got actionable, useful strategies. But please, bring others with you, pay it forward, pull them up and make them believe that they can do it too. Remember, I don't have a background in triathlon and I definitely never thought I would be writing a book after five Ironmans and 20+ marathons. We all need a little push every now and then, but when we are, it can lead to crazy twists and turns, and unbelievable experiences and accomplishments. You can do it. You are capable.

All the best in your triathlon journey,
Scott

APPAREL & EQUIPMENT

These are my best recommendations on triathlon apparel and equipment. They are based on my own personal experiences and what I've seen with clients. By no means am I a "professional triathlon apparel-testing guru." In the grand scheme of things, my knowledge may be somewhat limited because there are so many choices out there. I only know what's worked best for me and what I believe to be true. As with anything, do your own individual homework before making any major apparel or equipment decisions.

If you want to DO a triathlon, this is what you need:

- ✓ Wetsuit (unless you're in a warm weather climate)

Recommendation: ANY. Shop around online and find one that works in your budget.

- ✓ Swim Goggles

Recommendation: TYR

- ✓ Bike

Recommendation: ANY. You can do a triathlon on anything from a mountain bike to a less-expensive road bike. I would recommend buying through your local bike shop because the fit is going to be as important as the cost. The last thing you want to do is buy online and have a bike that fits you incorrectly.

- ✓ Bike Helmet

Recommendation: BELL

- ✓ Running Shoes

Recommendation: Asics or Mizuno. My clients have had the best results in these shoes and they're the brands I ran in for my first few years in endurance sports. They may not be the lightest shoes but they are durable and fit well.

APPAREL & EQUIPMENT

If you are brand new and you only want to DO a triathlon, these are the bare bones goods that you will need. This assumes you'll either be riding a bike with regular pedals or one with toe cages. But these are the *essentials*.

If you want to do a triathlon WELL, this is what you need:

- ✓ Wetsuit (assuming it's legal in your race)

Recommendation: TYR, Orca or 2XU

- ✓ Swim Goggles

Recommendation: TYR

- ✓ Bike Helmet

Recommendation: BELL

- ✓ Triathlon Bike

Recommendation: FELT or Cervelo. Felt is an American company that makes great bikes for the price point. My first triathlon bike was a Felt. Cervelo makes a great bike too.

- ✓ Bike Shoes (to use with your clipless pedals)

Recommendation: ANY. Make sure they're comfortable.

- ✓ Running Shoes

Recommendation: Asics, Mizuno or Newton. I've fallen in love with Newton running shoes. They're not for everyone, as they put you more on your forefoot when you run, but they're light and durable.

APPAREL & EQUIPMENT

- ✓ Triathlon Suit

Recommendation: ANY. Make sure it's comfortable.

- ✓ Performance Nutrition

Recommendation: AdvoCare + Hammer Nutrition. My personal favorites from AdvoCare are Rehydrate, Rehydrate Gels and Spark. Post Workout Recovery and Nighttime Recovery will help to reduce muscle soreness. I use Endurolytes in powder and pills from Hammer Nutrition (especially if it's hot).

These recommendations are for someone who may be new to triathlon but still would like a decent finishing time, or an experienced triathlete who would like to finish faster. Upgrading to a triathlon bike with clipless pedals will add a great deal of speed by itself and the addition of a triathlon suit will make sure you're more comfortable and aerodynamic. Performance nutrition helps fuel your body to be its best in training and racing.

If you want to perform your absolute BEST in triathlon, this is what you need:

- ✓ Wetsuit (assuming it's legal in your race)

Recommendation: TYR. You may want to look into a sleeveless wetsuit. You'll lose a bit of buoyancy but you'll have increased range of motion in your shoulders.

- ✓ Swim Goggles

Recommendation: TYR

- ✓ Aero Bike Helmet

Recommendation: Giro

- ✓ Carbon Triathlon Bike

Recommendation: Cervelo. Most of the high-end carbon triathlon bikes are good but I personally love Cervelo. Everyone I know has never had a bad thing to say about it and mine fits me perfectly. I've had zero mechanical issues.

- ✓ Bike Shoes

Recommendation: ANY. Make sure they're comfortable.

- ✓ Racing Wheels

APPAREL & EQUIPMENT

Recommendation: ZIPP or HED. *Any* race wheels are better than no race wheels and you will quickly see that the deeper the dish, the more expensive the wheel. I've never personally ridden a disc wheel and I normally don't recommend it because it it's windy, you're going to be blown all over the road.

NOTE – if you don't want to throw down the money to buy race wheels, some bike and triathlon shops will also have them available for rent on race day.

- ✓ Lightweight Running Shoes or Racing Flats

Recommendation: Newtons, Zoot or any type of racing flat. Weight becomes the most important thing here but, whatever you choose, make sure you've tested it out in training.

- ✓ Triathlon Suit

Recommendation: ANY. Make sure it's comfortable.

- ✓ Performance Nutrition

Recommendation: AdvoCare + Hammer Nutrition. My personal favorites from AdvoCare are Rehydrate, Rehydrate Gels and Spark. Add in Arginine Extreme to enhance blood flow. Post Workout Recovery and Nighttime Recovery will help to reduce muscle soreness. I use Endurolytes in powder and pills from Hammer Nutrition (especially if it's hot).

Long Distance Triathlon Tips and Strategies

If you're someone who is training for a 70.3 or an Ironman, you'll get a lot out of this video. It's a collection of insights for some of my best clients after they had gotten done completing a 70.3, on their way to Ironman Canada and Ironman Wisconsin.

Free Instant Access at:
OutperformTheNorm.com/books

TERMINOLOGY

<u>Active Recovery:</u> Recovery done in between interval sets in a single workout, or recovery done in between difficult workouts. The recovery is light, aerobic activity that is meant to flush out the lactic acid accumulation that results from hard exercise and speed up the rebuilding process.

<u>Anaerobic Threshold:</u> The point in which your body is producing lactic acid faster than it can clear it, or the point in which you become breathless during exercise. Think of pouring oil into a funnel--Anaerobic Threshold is the point that the oil starts to back up in the funnel and won't drain as fast as you're pouring it.

<u>Cardiovascular Drift:</u> An increase in heart rate at a constant exercise intensity that usually results from dehydration, fatigue, and the redistribution of blood flow from non-working to working muscles. This is more pronounced in hot weather (and humidity), as well as in longer races (>90 minutes).

<u>Clearance Run:</u> A type of active recovery--a run done in between difficult runs to keep the body fresh and sharp. These are short, aerobic efforts that will prime the body for the key workouts of the week.

Commitment: Making a promise to yourself that something will get done. You can make a commitment to others as a way to strengthen the action, but at the end of the day it all starts with you, and what someone else says or does has no bearing on your actions and level of commitment.

Diet: A word that should be stricken from the English vocabulary. It typically implies some type of restriction for a finite period of time, which never, EVER, works. Yes, it may work short term, but after that period of time passes that you dieted for, what happens? You spiral into utter confusion and slowly, but surely, you gain all the weight back and then some. It's a virtual certainty. Only when a commitment to a lifestyle happens will you ever achieve lasting results.

Dynamic Stretching: Controlled movements done before exercise to loosen up the muscles. This is not ballistic stretching. The movements take the muscles through the complete range of motion. Key areas are the hips, hamstrings, trunk, and shoulders.

Electrolytes: Magnesium, Calcium, Sodium, Potassium. All of these things are lost in sweat and must be replaced. Use Rehydrate by AdvoCare or Endurolytes by Hammer Nutrition (either in capsule or powder form) to help replace these during exercise. These minerals can make or break your performance and should not be overlooked.

Foundation Run: Foundation Runs are very useful in developing your aerobic system and strengthening your body's connective tissue. They are what most people refer to as "Long

TERMINOLOGY

Slow Distance." They build a strong "Foundation" on your house and give you the ability to raise a higher "ceiling" later on.

Gray Area: Stay away from this area at all costs! Too difficult to be completely aerobic but not difficult enough to be a Tempo Workout and pull up the Anaerobic Threshold. Use a heart rate monitor and you should be able to avoid this...

Heart Rate: The best indicator of intensity during exercise. Period. Heart rate tells you what the body is experiencing--pace tells you what the body is accomplishing. The body will accomplish nothing if you're not able to monitor what it is experiencing.

Heart Rate Monitor: A window into the physiological stress on the body, or in plain English--a tool that allows you to monitor your effort during exercise instantaneously. It is your body's speedometer. This is one of the most important investments you can make if you're looking to improve your fitness. Don't overlook it.

Interval Workout: An interval workout consists of high intensity "work" periods, followed by lower intensity "recovery" periods. Tough workouts to do--mentally and physically. But, if structured properly in a program, they are very useful in boosting fitness and giving you that added "edge" on race day.

Lactate Threshold: The point in which your body is producing lactic acid faster than it can clear it, or the point in which you become breathless during exercise. Think of pouring oil into a funnel--Lactate Threshold is the point that the oil starts to back up in the funnel and won't drain as fast as you're pouring it. The terms Lactate Threshold and Anaerobic Threshold are often used synonomously.

Lactic Acid: Think of this as a poison that seeps into your body during hard exercise. You can tolerate it in small amounts, but if there's too much of it, it'll ruin you. You can build up your tolerance to lactic acid through Interval Workouts and Tempo Workouts.

Limiters: Areas for improvement that are keeping an athlete from achieving peak performance. These can be mental or physical, but unless they're improved, the athlete will never achieve their full potential. Remember--the true champion will spend more time working on weakness than showing off strength.

Maximum Heart Rate: The highest heart rate (maximum exertion) your body can have during exercise. It is neither practical, nor necessary, to actually do a test to find out this number. It is usually an estimation based off of one's anaerobic threshold. If you have a very high fitness level you'll be in the ballpark of your maximum heart rate on tough interval workouts, but you'll still not actually approach it.

Mental Edge: Your ability to overcome your own demons, persevere and get the job done--to the best of your ability. People that are mentally strong have confidence, self-belief, a willingness to accept failure, and a burning desire to succeed. In sports, this is often this difference maker and it is too often overlooked as an integral aspect of training.

Metabolism: Your internal furnace, or how quickly your body burns calories at rest. Contrary to what people may think, this IS changeable based on lifestyle, nutrition, and exercise. Rid yourself of the notion that you were born with either a slow or fast metabolism. You CAN train your metabolism to work for you!

Muscular Endurance: The ability of a muscle to repeatedly contract over a sustained period of time and a strong resistance to fatigue during exercise. This is often a limiter for people that are in their first 1-3 years of endurance sports.

Negative Split: Workout or race where the second half is faster than the first half...meaning you're getting faster with time.

Periodization: The manipulation of frequency, intensity, and duration in a training program to achieve optimal performance for a "peak" race. Periods of training are divided up into Macrocycles, Mesocycles, and Microcycles. Almost all coaches work with some form of periodization, yet there are still large variations in what combination of the three variables will yield the best results.

Pickups: Gradual accelerations that can be inserted into the warmup of a Tempo Run, and periodically in an advanced Foundation Run (to keep the legs turning over during a long run). Pickups are guided more by feel, but they are accelerations of no more than 20-30 seconds that are similar to "controlled sprints."

Process Cues: Cues that you focus on during the race to help you achieve your best performance. These are things that are rehearsed in training and are conscious self-talk thoughts on specific movements. For example, a runner may focus on staying relaxed in the shoulders and light on the feet. A cyclist may focus on pedaling circles, and a swimmer may focus on an early elbow bend.

Progression Run: A Progression Run is the next step up, or progression, from a Foundation Run. The basis of the run is that it is still part of your aerobic development, but you are progressing the intensity over time. These workouts are very useful in improving long-distance race performance because they teach you to run faster as the body gets tired.

Recovery Drink: Typically contain a 3:1 or 4:1 ratio of carbs:protein and plenty of electrolytes. They are best taken within 30 minutes of exercise--the sooner the better. There are many good recovery drinks out there--my favorite is *Post Workout Recovery* by AdvoCare.

Running Drills: My favorites are 1) high knees, 2) butt kickers and 3) strides. See the Video Vault on how to perform these running drills.

Running Economy: The oxygen cost to your body when running. Running economy can change at different paces. Think of it like your car's miles per gallon--it may guzzle gas in

TERMINOLOGY

the city but be more efficient on the highway. The speeds that you typically train at can have a large effect on your running economy and where you become most efficient.

Sacrifice: Giving up, replacing, or losing something in the favor of something else. Some type of sacrifice is always necessary to attain a goal, and the higher the level of goal, the greater the sacrifice. Determining whether one is willing to sacrifice is a key determinant of achievement.

Static Stretching: Isolating a muscle and holding a continuous stretch for 20-60 seconds. Very beneficial for flexibility POST-exercise. More studies are coming out that show static stretching pre-exercise can make the body *more* susceptible to injury. Therefore, stick to dynamic stretching during the warmup, and static stretching during the cooldown.

Stepback Week: A week of lower volume/lower intensity training that allow the body to recover from harder preceding weeks. It also allows the body to prepare for an increase in volume/intensity in the following weeks. Stepback weeks are a necessary component to prevent overtraining.

Strides: From a standing position, start running and gradually accelerate up to top speed...hold this for a brief moment and let your body "glide" until you've slowed to a walk. Rest and repeat. You'll need about 60 yards to be able to appropriately do strides. You can build up to 8-10 strides and you'll usually do them before an Interval Workout, or after a Foundation Run or Progression Run. Strides SHOULD NOT fatigue you. They build neuromuscular speed--thus making you feel sharp and fast.

Stride Length: The distance of each stride while running. Stride length can be improved greatly by bounding drills up hills. Forceful push off (hip extension) is a key driving factor to having a long stride length. Elites can have up to 1.0-1.3x their height in stride length (Wow!), whereas normal runners will be about .6-.8x their height. These numbers indicate that, even if it doesn't seem like it, faster runners do a tremendous job of pushing off while running.

Stride Rate: The number of footstrikes you take per minute while running. Most elite runners will take 90+, us ordinary mortals should shoot for 85-90. You can count your number of footstrikes (I typically count for 15 seconds and multiply by 4). It is very economical and efficient to run at a high stride rate and it should be practiced often on slight downhills of a -1% to -3% grade.

Tempo Run: A sustained effort at, or slightly above, one's anaerobic threshold. This is a key workout to improve the body's ability to tolerate lactic acid accumulation and maintain a consistently fast pace during fatigue.

ABOUT THE AUTHOR

SCOTT WELLE is a #1 international best selling author, speaker and founder of Outperform The Norm, a global movement that coaches athletes and business leaders to raise their game and perform at the highest level.

While the rest of the competition is playing not to lose, Scott teaches people to play to win. His proprietary "Commit / Attack / Conquer" formula ensures people fall asleep at night knowing they are making the most of their precious days on this planet. For this, Fox 9 in Minneapolis-St Paul has called him a *"Motivational Expert."*

Scott has always loved sports but felt he underperformed early in his career by not mastering the "mental game." After graduating with his Master's degree in Sport Psychology, he made it his life's mission to coach people to higher levels of performance and not let others repeat his mistakes. Throughout this process, he's realized how the same mental principles that allow athletes to be successful will allow business leaders to achieve exceptional results, and this formed the foundation for Outperform The Norm.

Now, Scott's eight best selling books, articles, videos and podcasts inspire hundreds of thousands of people worldwide and students in over 35 countries have taken his online courses. He is an adjunct professor at St. Olaf University and serves on advisory committees of three national level organizations. He regularly coaches top performing executives, sales professionals and entrepreneurs, as well as elite athletes, all with one common goal: to OUTPERFORM.

Scott enjoys pushing his own physical and mental limits, completing five Ironman triathlons, 29 marathons, R2R2R (47 miles back and forth through the Grand Canyon) and a 100-mile ultra marathon run. He is very close with his brother, Jason. Together they "plod" at least one marathon together each year, laughing the whole way.

Please visit him at ScottWelle.com.

ALSO BY SCOTT WELLE

OUTPERFORM THE NORM

Health. Happiness. High Performance.

OutperformTheNorm.com/books

**The 50 Best Tips EVER
for Running Fitter, Faster and Forever**

OutperformTheNorm.com/books

EXCERPT

(from The 50 Best Tips EVER for Running)

I tried everything. Changing shoes, changing nutrition, changing my running form and changing my training plan. I even prayed to the running gods! It didn't matter. Every time I'd bolt out the door for a run something new would hurt. I was a broken down, frustrated runner. The most common pain was in my calves and I used to joke that you could flip a coin for which one was going to hurt that day. Because of this, I wasn't getting fitter and my times certainly weren't getting faster (in fact, they were getting slower). Running wasn't fun.

Even though it seems like only yesterday, that was five years ago. At the time, the more things I changed, the more it felt like I was wasting my time. But slowly my running started to improve. My body felt better...and healthier. I got fitter...and I got faster. I'm an experimenter at heart – I love tinkering with different things and trying to figure out not only what works...but what works the BEST. In this case, I was after the secret sauce of running.

What I came to realize is that your ability to be fit, run far and remain injury free is both simple, yet amazingly complex (how's that for an oxymoron?). What I mean when I say this is that there are only a select few SIMPLE things that need to be executed to run efficiently and effectively. Let's call these the basic fundamentals, if you will. Do these things and you'll run well. The complexity comes from the fact that there are actually a few things in *multiple categories* that need to be performed if you're looking to run your personal best. And these categories are Mentality, Muscles, Movements, Mobility and Metabolics.

What came from my own tinkering was the formation of the comprehensive running system on the market, Run M5. I don't say this be arrogant – I say it because there are no other systems that combine all these elements. This book is the condensed version of the 50 best tips EVER for running fitter, faster and forever. These tips were created based on the most common questions that I get from runners, whether it is a client of mine or somebody asking a question after I've conducted a running seminar. If certain questions are always coming up, it's obvious there are myths and misinformation permeating throughout the running communities. This book is my best attempt at setting the record straight.

Before we dig in, I want to make sure we're clear on a couple things:

First, I'm not an elite runner. In fact, my current PR in a marathon in 3:08:09. For some of you reading this, that will seem fast. For others, that will seem obnoxiously slow. Judge it however you want to but what I can tell you is that I didn't grow up running. I grew up playing football, basketball and golf (I only ran if someone was chasing me!). I caught the running bug later in graduate school, and although I've read all the major books on running, I've had no formal run coaching. I'm a self-taught runner who spent his first 5 years constantly injured and spinning his wheels. But, now, I've now run 5+ years with NO injuries and I'm only getting fitter and faster with age.

I believe I've found the secret sauce.

I say this because these principles haven't just worked on me. I've been blessed and fortunate to coach 50+ athletes from

5k's, to ultra marathons, to Ironmans, with 98% of them setting a personal best. This system WORKS. And it works because the athletes become more economical (they waste less energy), more efficient (they get injured less) and more effective (they train and race smarter).

OUTPERFORM THE NORM
for Student Athletes

Perform Your Best in Sports, School and LIFE

OutperformTheNorm.com/books

EXCERPT

(from Chapter 9 of Outperform The Norm for Student Athletes)

Think about the last time you were nervous for a game or competition – was it a meaningless scrimmage or something significant? I already know the answer – it is the latter. Whether it's a test, a video game, or a championship game, if you don't care about the outcome, you won't get nervous for it.

Only meaningful things make us nervous. Only big events bring butterflies.

That might sound obvious to you but the first step to harnessing your nervous energy is to pay attention to your *interpretation* of the nervousness. Most people look at nerves as though there's something wrong with them if they're feeling that way. They think it's going to hurt their performance. They automatically associate sweaty palms, a dry mouth and butterflies in their stomach as negatives. IT'S NOT. *Everybody* gets nervous, even elite and professional athletes.

Outperformers, on the other hand, look at nerves as a GOOD thing that's going to help their performance. They flip the switch and say to themselves, *"I can't wait to compete in this BIG game!"* or *"This is GREAT how much nervous energy I have!"* It sounds strange to look at it this way but that's the interpretation and internal dialogue that happens with great athletes.

Next, identify your ZOF (Zone of Optimal Functioning). This was also discussed in the last chapter *Getting In The Zone* and it's the level of arousal, anxiety, and nervous energy you like to feel during games and competitions. Some people like to feel like they're bouncing off the walls; others want to be left alone to stay very calm and relaxed. There isn't a right and a wrong way. It's simply YOUR way and it's critically important to find your ZOF where you perform and function your best.

To go a little deeper, the physiology of nerves happens mostly in the sympathetic nervous system, which is why we are consciously manipulating it to find our ZOF.[14] If you are someone that functions better at the lower end of the arousal scale, focus on taking long, slow, deep breaths. Also make an intentional effort to slow down your pre-competition movements. Walk slower and talk slower. Be more deliberate in your actions. Doing these things will help you feel more relaxed. If you're a higher-strung person you want to do the exact opposite. Be very purposeful and energetic in your movements. Let the energy move you. Fast-paced music is also a great thing to use, as it's typically easier to increase your arousal level with music than it is to decrease it.

Lastly, try to remove the outcomes and focus on the processes. When we get really nervous about ANYTHING, it's almost always because we're fixated on the OUTCOME. We worry:

"What grade am I going to get on the test?"

"Am I going to make the team?"

"Are we going to win or lose this championship game?"

Outcome. Outcome. Outcome. Our nerves are tied to results, which in sports, usually translates to winning and losing. You probably remember from the *Owning and Smashing Your Goals* chapter that we only have indirect control over outcomes in our lives. We need to refocus on controlling the controllables and one thing that you can *always* control is the process. So, before a big competition, the processes are the actions that are going to facilitate the outcome. These are always things over which you have 100% control.

For example, if you're a sprinter, instead of being nervous about winning or losing the race, your process might be to focus on a strong push off out of the blocks, a big powerful arm swing, keeping the heap down early, and staying tall as you near the finish line. All of these different processes are 100% in your control and they remove you from worrying about the outcome.

OUTPERFORM THE NORM
for Sales

The 50 Best Tips EVER for Successful Selling

OutperformTheNorm.com/books

OUTPERFORM THE NORM
for Network Marketing

Six Steps to Six Figures This Year

OutperformTheNorm.com/books

Printed in Great Britain
by Amazon